SATISH KUMAR was born in Rajasthan in India in 1936. When he was only nine years old, he renounced the world and joined the wandering brotherhood of Jain monks. Dissuaded from his path by an inner voice at the age of eighteen, he became a campaigner for land reform, working to turn Gandhi's vision of renewed India and a peaceful world into reality.

Fired by the example of Bertrand Russell, he undertook an 8,000-mile peace pilgrimage, walking from India to Europe and then in America without any money, through deserts, mountains, storms and snow. It was an adventure during which he was thrown into jail in France, faced a loaded gun in America—and delivered packets of 'peace tea' to the leaders of the four nuclear powers.

In 1973 he settled in England, taking on the editorship of *Resurgence* magazine, and has been the Editor ever since. He is the guiding spirit behind a number of ecological, spiritual and educational ventures in Britain. He founded the Small School in Hartland, a pioneering secondary school which brings into its curriculum ecological and spiritual values. In 1991, Schumacher College, a residential international centre for the study of ecological and spiritual values, was founded, of which he is the Director of Programmes.

Following Indian tradition, in his fiftieth year, he undertook another pilgrimage: again carrying no money, he walked to the holy places of Britain—Glastonbury, Canterbury, Lindisfarne and Iona. Meeting old friends and making new ones along the way, this pilgrimage was a celebration of his love of life and nature.

In July 2000 Satish Kumar was awarded an Honorary Doctorate in Education from the University of Plymouth. In July 2001 he was awarded an Honorary Doctorate in Literature from the University of Lancaster. And in November 2001 he was presented with the Jamnalal Bajaj International Award for Promoting Gandhian Values Abroad.

His autobiography, *No Destination*, also published by Green Books, has been reprinted many times in several editions. It was published in the USA in 2000 by William Morrow under the title *Path Without Destination*.

"England's one prophet, William Blake, wrote that 'Everything that lives is holy.' This is the fundamental teaching of Gaia, the new vision of Earth as a single living whole. We are most blessed in having in Satish Kumar a teacher of this new understanding of the truth, both new and age-old, of the one indivisible life that sustains us all. We in the materialist modern West have to relearn truths we have long forgotten. Satish brings from his traditional Jain background in India—and also from the modern India of Mahatma Gandhi, Vinoba Bhave and living examples like Vandana Shiva—a message that speaks to a generation eager to discover a way of life that can bring healing to our Earth and its people in the twenty-first century."—**Kathleen Raine, poet and Blake scholar**

"At a time when economic exclusion of globalisation and the cultural exclusion of terrorism and fundamentalism are destroying the very fabric of our societies, our collective existence by the 'us' vs 'them' culture, which treats the 'other' as enemy, and creates fear and hatred, Satish Kumar offers us the gift of *So Hum**—'You Are, Therefore I Am'. His mental journey and his inspirations need to become everyone's inspiration to help us to move from violence to non-violence, from greed to compassion, from arrogance to humility."—**Vandana Shiva, author of** *Staying Alive*

"Satish Kumar is a planter of acorns."—**Jonathon Porritt, author, and co-founder and Programme Director of Forum for the Future**

*See page 10

Praise for Satish Kumar's autobiography, *No Destination*

"If there is any single book which exudes both wisdom as well as tranquillity, then it is *No Destination*."—**Victor Papanek, author of *Design for the Real World***

"Satish Kumar is, for me, the sage of the deep ecology movement. His many enterprises—the journal *Resurgence*, the Schumacher Lectures, the Small School, Schumacher College—have all been successful because they are based on the same spiritual core, clear vision and selfless non-attachment. This fascinating book shows us how Satish Kumar became who he is today."—**Fritjof Capra, author of *The Tao of Physics* and *The Web of Life***

"Satish Kumar is among the most important educators of the 20th century. His lifelong odyssey adds a compelling flesh-and-blood reality to the wisdom of the East."—**Theodore Roszak, author of *The Making of a Counter Culture***

"Satish Kumar's unique story is stranger than fiction. The life of this vigorous, wise, compassionate and humble man is an example to all of us about how to make the most of our gifts and create our own opportunities to serve humanity's future. I am honoured to be his friend and colleague."—**Hazel Henderson, author of *Building a Win-Win World* and *Creating Alternative Futures***

"Reading this book, you will have the rare pleasure of meeting a warm and witty, thoroughly genuine man, and one whose inspiration will not fail to move you."—**Kirkpatrick Sale, author of *The Green Revolution* and *Rebels Against the Future***

"A remarkable story—a biography, in its way, of the modern alternative community. . . . Describes episodes in his life that many readers would dismiss as fables were they not true."—**David Nicholson-Lord, *The Independent***

"One of the few life-changing books I have ever read. I wish everyone would read it."—**Thomas Moore, author of *Care of the Soul***

YOU ARE
Therefore
I AM

A Declaration of Dependence

Satish Kumar

with illustrations by Truda Lane

Green Books

First published in 2002
by Green Books Ltd
Foxhole, Dartington
Totnes, Devon TQ9 6EB

Cover design by Rick Lawrence

Illustrations © Truda Lane
'Sowing the Seed' poem © Wendell Berry
'Because We Are' poem © Rosalind Brackenbury

Text printed by Biddles Ltd, Guildford, Surrey
on Five Seasons 100% recycled paper

British Library Cataloguing in Publication Data
available on request

ISBN 1 903998 18 2

Contents

Acknowledgements

This book has come into being because my daughter Maya offered to transcribe it for me: this is how the oral culture of India has often operated. The book has therefore been a joint project. Maya helped to make some of my Indian experiences more relevant to a Western reader, and I thank Maya for her help and good humour.

Then I would like to thank my two friends, John Lane and Chris Cullen, who in their busy lives made time to read the first draft and give many useful and helpful comments and corrections. I am indebted to both of them.

I would also like to express my gratitude to my wife June, who co-authored some of Part Three, helped me to remember missing stories, and whose sensitive editing gave order to the book.

If you are a poet, you will see clearly that there is a cloud floating in this sheet of paper. Without a cloud, there will be no rain; without rain, the trees cannot grow; and without trees, we cannot make paper. The cloud is essential for the paper to exist. If the cloud is not here, the sheet of paper cannot be here either.

—Thich Nhat Hanh

Foreword

THIS BOOK IS a journey of the mind. In it I trace the sources of inspiration which formed my understanding of the world as a network of multiple and diverse, yet interrelated relationships.

The book is written in four parts. The first describes my memories of conversations with my mother, my teacher and my guru, all of whom were deeply religious, and gave me a strong spiritual beginning. The second part recounts my time with Vinoba Bhave, an Indian sage; Krishnamurti, a prophet of freedom; Bertrand Russell, a philosopher of scientific rationalism; Martin Luther King, a liberator of the oppressed; and Fritz Schumacher, an ecological economist. These five great activists and thinkers inspired me to engage with social, spiritual and political issues. In the third part I narrate my travels in India, which have continued to nourish my mind and reconnect me with my roots.

The fourth part brings together a world-view based in relationships and connections in all things rather than based in the philosophy of dualism, division and separation of which René Descartes, perhaps, was the father. Tragedies such as the 11 September 2001 attack on the twin towers of New York, which I witnessed, and other international conflicts—the arms race, ecological degradation and social injustice—are rooted in the Cartesian doubts, in dualism, individualism and all the other 'isms'. The seeds of dualistic thought are to be found in Descartes' famous dictum 'I think, therefore I am': *Cogito, ergo sum*.

However, I hold an emergent world-view, encapsulated in a Sanskrit dictum, *So Hum*, well known in India but not in the West. It has become my mantra, the mantra of non-dualistic and unfragmented relationships. I translate *So Hum* as 'You are, therefore I am': *Estis, ergo sum*. This mantra underpins all the experiences brought together in this book.

During this intellectual journey my mind has been greatly nourished and fascinated by three great fountains of wisdom. The first of them is India herself. Even though I was born and brought up there, India is still, for me, an enigma. I am often shocked, surprised and mystified by her. The idea of India is as much intriguing and inspiring to me as the land and culture itself. So this book is partly about India.

Secondly, the landscape of my mind is painted by the colours of the Jain religion. I have recently noticed how often I draw from the Jain stories and connections I thought I had left behind so long ago. So this book is also about Jain principles and precepts.

Thirdly, I am at a confluence of East and West. Having lived in England for the past thirty years, I am as much influenced by the West as I am by the East. My mind is shaped by a synthesis of East and West and yet I pursue the path of a free spirit which goes beyond geographical, religious and cultural boundaries.

I come from an oral culture. All the conversations I have recorded in this book are from memory. I have not kept a diary, nor written records of any kind whatsoever. I have used speech marks only to make it easier for the reader. I make no claims that this is a verbatim report of what was said—it is not. It is simply how I understood at the time and remember it now.

Satish Kumar
Hartland
15th February 2002

Whereof one cannot speak, one must remain silent.
—Ludwig Wittgenstein

PART ONE

Encounters *with* Meaning

Animals are our kith and kin.
—Bhagwan Parshwanath

There is no separation between the observer and the observed, between the subject and the object; they are a seamless continuum.

—J. Krishnamurti

Chapter 1

Learning from Nature

"Nature is the greatest teacher," said my mother while we were walking from home to our farm.

"Greater than the Buddha," she continued, "for even he learned from nature. He became enlightened while sitting under a tree, contemplating on the compassionate, generous, ever-giving tree. While observing the banyan tree under which he was sitting, the Buddha realised that the fulfilment and self-realisation of the tree was in its being that which it is, never trying to be anything other than a tree. As tree it was always available to those who came to it: the birds could nest in it, the animals could rest under its cool shade, and everyone could benefit from its fruit."

I was only eight years old, listening to my mother, and yet this was something I could understand. She would talk to me in more or less the same way that she would talk to my older sisters and brothers. For her, I was not 'a child—an underdeveloped adult'. She always talked to me about matters of great substance.

Yet Mother was an illiterate woman: she could not read, nor write. She could not even sign her name, and on a document she would put her thumbprint. But she was both deeply religious and an intuitive philosopher.

My mother, whose name was Anchi Devi, was born in 1900, in the small town of Momasar in Rajasthan. Her parents were farmers, so she grew up on the land. Therefore, her religion, her spirituality, her philosophy and her way of life were part of her experiences, rather than a result of any formal education.

Mother was short and slim with bright eyes. The wrinkles on her kind and thoughtful face were clear evidence of an active and eventful life. She wore traditional clothes: an earth-coloured skirt with tie-dyed red circles on it, full and long, a black blouse and a dark brown cotton wrap which went over her shoulders and head, and veiled her forehead. All her clothes were woven, dyed and stitched locally in our town. She adhered to the Jain religion. Everything she did was underpinned by a religious view of life.

My father, Hiralal Sethia, was also Jain. His family lived fifteen miles away in another small town, Sri Dungargarh. His parents were merchants, trading in grain. What my mother's family grew, my father's family traded.

"After only three or four years of our marriage I felt a sense of loss," my mother recounted, "I didn't know what to do with myself—no land, no trees, no animals. So I persuaded your father to purchase some land. At first he was reluctant, but when he realised that we could have our own milk, butter and ghee, fresh fruit and vegetables, his taste buds persuaded him, and I was so happy."

This was very unusual. Generally speaking, Jains do not farm. They believe that farming is not conducive to their practice of non-violence, which is a central principle of the Jain religion. In their eyes the use of animals, even for ploughing, is a form of violence. While cultivating the land we may harm insects. Jains also avoid using honey because it deprives bees of their food. The use of silk and leather also involves violence to living creatures, and is therefore undesirable. But my mother had her own point of view in this matter. As long as we eat food, someone has to grow it, and therefore it is better to grow it ourselves, and grow it with care. In our family, as in all Jain families, we were strict vegetarians. No one dreamed of eating meat, as that would totally disqualify one from being Jain. But some Jains like my mother saw the violence of farming as unavoidable and acceptable. Non-violence to her was refraining from avoidable violence and from the intention to harm any creatures unnecessarily, or due to lack of care.

LIFE FOR MOTHER was a tapestry made up of millions of small acts, but each one was an essential contribution to the realisation of that tapestry. She did not believe in great acts of heroism; she believed in small actions performed with great love and imagination.

Mother gave to all material things a high value; she saw matter as the vehicle of the spirit and therefore she handled all things with reverence.

When I look back to my childhood I realise she was one of many women whose life and soul were formed and informed by Jain teachings. Mother believed that the whole of life should be lived as a spiritual practice, as a meditation. Self-realisation is not something for tomorrow, not somewhere far away in the distance; it is here and now in all our actions, guided by reverence for matter, reverence for work, reverence for life.

Being a Jain family, we did not live as isolated individuals; we were not taught to stand on our own feet and fend for ourselves. Ours was a relationship of mutuality: mutual sharing, mutual caring, no privacy, no private possessions, no private wealth; everything belonged to the family. This was particularly evident in Mother's life; she found her fulfilment and happiness in taking care of the family and being an inseparable part of the community.

Our family lived in a house built of local stone, around two courtyards. The inner courtyard was connected to an outer courtyard where cows were milked, herbs were grown, rainwater was collected, guests were accommodated, and corn was dried, threshed and winnowed. The whole set-up was very simple. Everything was in good order and seemed amply sufficient for our needs. The family business, which was based on trade in grain and jute, brought enough income in cash to keep the needs of the family well supplied. We were not rich, we were not poor, and we never thought of these categories.

The collection of the monsoon rainwater was part of our psyche. In the courtyard was a covered water tank, in which we collected the rainwater from the roofs of our house. This was as integral a part of our home as the grain store or the kitchen. The tank held all our drinking water for the entire year and never failed us.

Most of the households of the town had such water tanks. Harvesting of the monsoon rains was one of the major activities of the whole people of Rajasthan. Everywhere there were small water ponds, large water ponds, lakes, step wells, in the town, out of the town, between the fields—there were clusters of water stores wherever possible. There were wells ancient and modern, and new wells were always being dug. It seemed to me that the collection, conservation and preservation of monsoon water and the system to hold it was the most important communal preoccupation. There was a big water tank in the western part of our town. From that tank the water-men and women brought us our daily supply of washing water. Our share of water was one bucket per person per day. For Jains the wasting of water was a serious matter. Very early on my mother taught me a water sutra:

Waste not water
Nor ever spill it
Water is precious
Water is sacred
The way you use water is the measure of you
Water is the witness
Water is the judge
Your reputation rests on your careful use of water.

Mother would say, "The monsoon is a great friend of the people and the Earth. The monsoon comes once a year and brings the gift of water. Our task is to receive the gift with gratitude, to thank the rain god, and make use of water with care and reverence. Our task is to live in harmony with the monsoon and celebrate it. God Surya, the sun, and God Indra, the rain, are twin brothers and all life depends on them."

IN OUR COURTYARD there was a wild plum tree. It was a big tree and I loved climbing it. "When I came to this house, the courtyard was totally bare. So I planted the plum tree. Isn't it amazing that from the tiny seed I put in the soil such a lovely tree has grown." Once again Mother was in the mood to speak. She used the seed and the tree as a metaphor to illustrate her philosophy of change, of birth and death, of continuity and impermanence. She said, "As a seed is capable of becoming a tree, all human beings are also capable of realising their own full potential. In order for the seed to become a tree it must be planted in the soil—underground, in the dark, and almost forgotten. In relationship with the earth, the seed surrenders its separateness, its identity, its individuality, its ego. In fact, the seed allows itself to become one with the earth, only then its hidden energy bursts open and we see the green shoots emerging like a miracle."

I remember Mother talking like this. She used to go into a trance, and almost forget where she was and what she was doing. There was a kind of mystical quality about her, the like of which I have rarely experienced. When my mother spoke like that I would be transfixed too.

"Don't you think, my little one, it is a miracle? That tiny seed I planted thirty years ago has produced no one knows how many plums, and every one of those plums with a new seed in it. And all that from one seed. This is how I understand the meaning of eternity, and even the meaning of reincarnation." It was good that Mother did not muddy the waters by quoting any great scripture concerning eternity and reincarnation. Instead, she just pointed to our plum tree. Its fruit that I had eaten year after year, its branches on which I had climbed uncountable times, and the shade under which I had slept, were all so close to me.

"In the same way we human beings have to let go of our pride, our separateness, and not bother about our individual identity. If we immerse ourselves in the process of life, and trust the process of the universe, and identify ourselves with others, we can become the tree of a thousand branches and a million plums."

When I was eight years old, listening to Mother talk like this, I was a bit puzzled and said to her; "Of course I am a separate person, separate from you, from my brothers and sisters, from my friends. So how can I not be separate?"

Mother kept silent for a while. She went to the kitchen and I followed her. By now the rice was ready so she served it to me with vegetables and dhal. As I started to eat, I relaxed. My question was no longer occupying me. But Mother had not forgotten it. So she picked up the conversation at the right moment and said,

"You know, you are right, you do need a sense of the self, there is a place for it. Individuality and wholeness are complementary, not contradictory—like the seed needs the shell. Without the shell the seed is incapable of forming itself as a seed. Similarly, we humans have our identity giving us a sense of separateness, but a time comes when the seed needs to grow into a tree. That is the point of transformation. As the seed goes through transformation and realises itself as a tree, the shell is no longer necessary, and has to disintegrate in order for the seed to integrate with the other elements."

The rice and dhal Mother had served me was delicious, and I was more keenly absorbed in eating than in listening to her words. But somehow her words penetrated more deeply because I was not paying too much attention. Maybe, who knows, it was Mother's idea that she should speak to me like this while I was busy eating my lunch, and my sister Suraj was humming while washing the clothes.

Whether or not I was concentrating, there was no way to stop Mother "The seed comes from the tree and goes on to become a tree. The seedness of the seed is only transitory; there is the transition from seed to tree, so why get hooked on that? Similarly, we humans, each and every one of us, have our individuality, but this individuality is transitory. Our individuality may be more apparent than real. Would you exist without me, my son? Would you exist without the food you are eating? Would you exist without the ground on which you are sitting? Our individuality is dependent on others. Individuality is indivisible."

Although Mother was illiterate, she had learned many songs, poems and verses of our Jain religious literature by heart. One she recited was: "Souls render service to one another, and thus find salvation."

She related this verse to the seed and said, "Seed serves the earth, and the earth serves the seed. A tree sheds its leaves to the earth, and the earth gives nourishment to the roots of the tree. Thus souls are serving each other and being fulfilled."

"What about your lunch, Mother, aren't you going to eat?"
"No, no food today, I am fasting."

ANOTHER DAY, Mother and I were walking to our land. It was early in the morning. The vastness of red sky behind us was breathtaking. I asked, "Where does so much of this red colour come from?"

"It's a mystery, my boy, a mystery."

"It seems like someone has spilt tons and tons of red paint upon the sky!"

"Look at the beehive on that tree."

Mother was more captivated by the the bees than by the beauty of the the sky. "Bees go from flower to flower, taking only a little nectar here and a little nectar there, and doing no harm to the flower. How gentle and restrained they are. Never has a flower complained 'the honey bee came and stole away my nectar'. It is as if the bee knows it cannot exist without flowers, and the flower knows it cannot be without bees. But what do human beings do? When we start to extract the bounties of the earth, we know no limits, we go on taking and taking until the earth is depleted. What do the bees do with the nectar? They transform it into sweet, delicious and healing honey, while pollinating the plants. How many humans can do that? When we humans take the gifts of nature we cause so much waste and damage. If we could only learn from nature, we would take from the earth without violating the earth, and what we do take we would transform into something like honey, and return it as the tree's leaves return to the ground. Nature knows no waste."

OUR FARM WAS about three miles from our home, so generally it took over an hour to walk there in the morning, and an hour to walk back in the evening. Two hours of walking most days suited Mother very well.

"Your father used to come—when he did—on horseback, but I always said to him, why ride a horse when we have perfectly good legs to walk? And how would you like it, if a horse wanted to ride on you? Your father would laugh, but never use his legs." Normally Mother was quite complimentary about Father, but she wanted him to walk with her so that they had time to talk together. Mother rarely talked about trivial things, she liked to talk about meaning and mystery. But my father, a busy businessman, was more concerned about where the bread and butter was to come from rather than infinity and reincarnation.

I noticed that Mother had an expression of sorrow on her face when she mentioned my father. Father died when I was four years old, so I hardly knew him. I am my mother's son. I have always thought of and talked about Mother. I know of Father only by what Mother told me about him from time to time.

Sometimes people are puzzled that I speak so much about my mother. People say to me: In the West we don't talk about our mothers—it seems like you have a mother complex. I am not too worried about it. I learned so much from my mother that I like to acknowledge her influence on me.

It may be that, because our modern culture makes children reluctant to acknowledge and appreciate their mothers, many mothers have lost the sense of close connection with their children.

Father was involved in business, and not with the land. Therefore, he was less able to appreciate the beauty of nature. Mother found this awkward. However, Mother did appreciate Father's high-mindedness in business.

"He used to say," Mother recalled, " 'I am in business to make friends, and serve the community. Profit for me is by the way. One has to make profit and balance the books, otherwise the business will go bust, but profit is not the main motivation. Profit oils the wheels, but the purpose of operating the wheels is not to consume oil but to produce something for people. Profit is necessary but not primary. Making friends and forming relationships is much more fun. That is why I am in business.' " This made Mother very happy. She always believed in a simple way of life.

"Too many possessions take too much of your time," Mother believed. "You have to clean them, look after them, use them, store them; if you are always busy with material things, when do you have time for reflection, meditation and service to the community?"

So if Father did not bring much money home, that never bothered Mother, but Father not going for a walk in nature did disappoint her. As Mother was talking I could see her eyes getting moist; she was about to choke, but she did her best to hold her composure. It was clear that even though Father had died four years ago, Mother's feelings towards him were still tender. She quickly returned to her thoughts about walking.

For her, walking was the best way to exercise. It was better than yoga and better than running.

"Have you sweated today?" Mother would ask sister Suraj and me. "If not, go for a long brisk walk. Sweating cleanses the poison of the body and opens the pores. It keeps the skin healthy. Moreover, you get a free foot massage given to you by the sand. The herbs and grasses rubbing against your feet give you subtle doses of herbal treatment." She laughed.

For Mother, walking was much more than physical exercise, it was a meditation. Touching the earth, being connected to the soil, and taking every step consciously and mindfully, was supremely conducive to contemplation.

"Our Lord Mahavir, the great prophet of the Jain tradition, attained enlightenment while walking. This was dynamic meditation. Mahavir was meditating on self and world simultaneously, whereas in sitting meditation one is much more likely to focus on the self alone."

Mother was not self-centred. That is why she was out and about, flowing with the wind and finding spirit in nature. When I recall those days of walking with Mother, I realise that maybe that's why all my life I have enjoyed walking. Long-distance walking has presented no problems to me.

As I walked with her, Mother would teach me to breathe properly, and ask me to pay full attention to breathing. "Paying attention is meditation," Mother would say. She must have thought that if she could introduce the idea of walking and meditating into my mind at such an early age, I would never find them daunting. In particular I remember her saying, "Focus on the moment between the in-breath and the out-breath. Observe the subtle point when you are neither inhaling nor exhaling. No need to prolong that moment, no need to hold the breath. Just observe."

Mother had learned this technique from a nun who had practised meditation over twelve years. Jain nuns and monks walk barefoot every day, and use no other conveyance; therefore, they are the masters of walking meditation. I was lucky that I could learn meditation from my mother, without much effort.

"Breathing connects you with the world. You are sharing the same breath of life, the same air, with all humanity. You are connected with everyone through this invisible medium: you share the same breath with animals, birds, fish, plants—the entire universe. How wonderful that we are all connected through our breathing. Air knows no barriers, no boundaries, no distinctions, no separations. By paying attention to your breathing your sense of separateness is dissolved."

Once she had told me about this technique of breathing she would stop talking, and we would walk together for ten to twenty minutes in silence.

"Should I pay attention to my feet touching the earth or to my breathing? I can't do them both at once, can I?" I remember asking Mother.

"Yes, you can. Don't think about breathing, nor think about walking. Meditation is not about thinking on these things. Just let it happen." Only much later did I understand what she was saying: that meditation is not a self-conscious action, it is a way of letting go of thoughts, ideas, techniques and methods. Just to be—be aware, be attentive.

In the beginning, one learns the letters of the alphabet, but later on when one uses them in reading and writing one doesn't think about the alphabet, nor even of individual words. One flows with the language and the meaning; so with meditation.

Mother was very fond of the mantra 'Aum shanti, shanti, shanti'. She would chant this, sometimes aloud and at other times silently. "Sometimes my mind is too full of family affairs or farming matters. But when I use the mantra all thought-clouds disperse. Chanting is enchanting. It enables you to rise above, to transcend and be free of your mental maze. So whenever I am lost, the mantra helps me to be re-enchanted.

" 'Mantra' is a sacred word that has been charged and recharged by constant repetition. The more you chant the same mantra, the greater the potency. Mantra sweeps your mind clean. In Sanskrit 'man' means the mind and 'tra' means liberation. You liberate your mind through chanting. You become free of all mental tangles.

"This is why Hindus, Buddhists and Jains have used the technique of chanting mantras, and often share the same mantras."

Chapter 2

A Hindu Mind

ONE DAY AS Mother and I were returning from our fields, we met my brahmin teacher, Gopalji, a forty-year-old philosopher. Mother was very fond of him. Gopalji, though not a Jain, had much in common with my Mother in the way he saw the world. Outwardly, Gopalji looked very much like an orthodox brahmin. A well-dressed man, he wore a light saffron-coloured shirt (*kurta*) which was hand-spun and hand-woven in a nearby town. Over his shoulders he wore a white cotton shawl, upon which the sacred names of Radha and Krishna were printed, so that at no time should he forget that these gods were his true companions. His head was clean-shaven, apart from a long plait of black hair growing from his crown. His sandals, decorated with colourful threads, were handcrafted by the local shoemaker. He was tall and slim. We, the pupils of our little school, revered him greatly. He was our hero.

That day Gopalji was not feeling too well. He had caught a cold and was suffering from a headache. Mother invited him to come to our house so that she could give him a herbal drink. Neither tea nor coffee were ever used in our house. We had no kettle, no gas and no electricity. We did not use coal. For the Jains, coal-mining is a form of violence and to be avoided wherever possible.

The only fuel used in the house was wood and cow dung cake. The latter was considered particularly good and appropriate. In the desert, wood is scarce and cow dung is plentiful. Young boys and girls go around the grazing land and collect the dung, mix it with straw, shape the cakes and dry them in the sun. They would sell them to us. In addition, our own cows and buffalos produced dung which was turned into fuel. Dung was never used for compost: only the leaf and vegetable waste which the cows did not eat was put on the compost heap.

Some embers were always kept covered under ash, so that Mother could quickly revive the fire by adding the dung cakes to the embers. She boiled the water in a saucepan with cinnamon, dry ginger, cardamom, black pepper and a few leaves of *tulsi*, the Indian basil plant. Mother and Gopalji were totally devoted to this plant. The healing properties of tulsi are such that it helps to cure most ailments; it restores the self-renewing capacity of the body. The brew was never called tea, she called it *ukali*, which simply means 'spicy concoction'! Gopalji called it *yogi chai*.

In many homes in India a tulsi plant is an essential part of the household. It is believed that tulsi is a gift of Lord Shiva. It is not only a healing herb but also a deity. So every morning Mother would water the plant and then bow with both palms together, as a mark of her worshipful devotion. Gopalji believed that "The tulsi plant represents the entire vegetable kingdom. So by respecting tulsi you are paying homage to all plants. Likewise, the river Ganga represents all the waters of the world, so by making a pilgrimage to the Ganga we acknowledge the sacredness of water itself. The cow is holy. She is a symbol of the entire animal kingdom, and therefore all animals are sacred. The religious tradition has highlighted a particular plant, a particular animal or a particular bird as sacred only to remind us that all life is sacred."

As we drank ukali, Mother asked Gopalji why the mantra of 'Aum shanti shanti shanti' has become so universally recognised as the supreme mantra?

"If you chant this mantra, the very sound of it is enough to make you return to your centre. It is like the tulsi plant, the river Ganga, or the holy cow, it is a sacred word to make all words sacred.

"Aum is made up of three sounds, A, U, M. In Sanskrit, 'A' is the first and 'M' is the last letter of the alphabet, while U represents all the letters in between. So in the mantra Aum the entire structure of the language is distilled. It is the essence of all speech and of all existence, because according to our ancient tradition, existence itself emerged out of the sound 'Aum'.

"Goddess Uma, the consort of Lord Shiva, takes her name from the mantra Aum because she is the mother of all creation. Uma means mother. The mantra Aum is the Mother Principle. It means all, whole, complete. In Aum nothing is left out and everything is included."

While Gopalji was speaking Mother became totally absorbed, and her ukali was getting cold. I could see why Mother was so fond of Gopalji. He had such a clear and simple understanding of the matters which interested her.

Gopalji knew the *Bhagavad Gita*, which means Song of the Lord, one of India's great scriptures, by heart. He considered this "the most beautiful and eloquent poem ever written, where sound, mind and meaning converge." Gopalji was a Sanskrit scholar—although I don't know what difference that made, since Mother was as fluent in elucidating profound truths. Her illiteracy was no handicap. I was happy that I grew up in the company of such a mother and such a teacher.

Gopalji had not finished; he was enjoying himself in explaining the meaning of Aum to Mother.

"Aum is an affirmative mantra. It simply means 'yes'—yes to existence, yes to the sun and moon, yes to trees and rivers, yes to our friends and families, yes to you and me, yes to this brew we are drinking, yes to life and its beauty. It is a mantra of acceptance and openness, a mantra of positive thinking. We should chant it as often as we can. There is no fixed time for it. We don't have to sit cross-legged in a room to chant it; we can chant it while eating, bathing, walking—any time."

There was a pause. Mother poured more ukali into Gopalji's brass cup. In our house there was neither glass, china, nor plastic. Utensils were made of metal: brass, bronze and silver. Gopalji held the cup with a handkerchief, as there was no handle, to avoid being burned. He was savouring the drink. After allowing a brief breathing space Mother probed him further:

"Then how about shanti, shanti, shanti?"

It seemed as if Gopalji was waiting for such a question, and I was waiting too. Conversations between Mother and Gopalji were never boring.

" 'Shanti' in Sanskrit simply means peace. Peace is the ultimate discovery. Aren't we all searching for peace? When we are at peace we can find happiness and fulfilment."

"But why do we say it three times?" Mother asked.

"First of all we have to make peace with ourselves by accepting who we are. Each and everyone of us is a particular manifestation of the universal energy. We need to recognise that particularity and 'eachness'; that individuality. Often we have a habit of despising ourselves; 'I am not good enough' is a very common expression. This means I am at war with myself. Unless I make peace within, how can I make peace without? Without inner peace no outer peace can be realised.

"If our society is full of people who have self-respect, have no negative thoughts, and who have achieved a degree of peace of mind, then naturally they will not fear any 'enemies'. But if spiritually we have not been able to overcome our personal fears then it is very easy for governments and military leaders to encourage fear of an external enemy. Every day they tell us about the enemies. It suits them. It is in their interest. They want to create fear and keep us in fear. We are ruled by fear. Fear of our neighbours, fear of Hindus, fear of Muslims, fear of Christians, fear of other countries. We are all divided into different groups and fear somebody. We even fear our wife or husband, or fear our children. No wonder that we have leaders who spend much of the world's resources on armaments! It may not be so easy to see the connection between spiritual peace and political peace, between inner peace and world peace, but these two aspects are inseparable, totally interlinked.

"As long as we expect the world to change in our image, it will not change. The fear, the mistrust, the competitiveness, the insecurity that we see between nations and their leaders are rooted in us. The fear we have in our lives accumulates, and becomes national fear, national mistrust, national disunity, national insecurity.

"So unless we begin with ourselves we cannot achieve peace; we cannot even begin to understand what peace means.

"Once I have made peace with myself I have to make peace with the world. Like thinking 'I am not good enough', we also think 'My family is not good enough, my work is not good enough, society is not good enough, government is not good enough.' We are possessed with this negative force, and therefore there is no peace. So we need to recognise the essential and intrinsic goodness of the world, and build upon it the ideal world of our dreams. Then we will have world peace."

That was the time of the second world war, so he continued, "There is a false superiority from which we suffer: 'I am better than you, my religion is better than yours. My country is superior to yours' and so on. This kind of thinking produces inter-religious and international wars. Therefore, making peace with other races, religions and nations is included in this chant." Gopalji paused for a moment.

"And why do we invoke peace the third time?" Mother asked.

"When there is world peace, then we make peace with nature, with the cosmos, with the gods—with the universe. The world does not only consist of humans, and therefore we need to make peace with all life forms, going beyond the human world. The whole earth is one family—humans, animals, birds, plants—all are related, and therefore we chant 'peace' three times so that it prevails and permeates these three spheres, personal, social and cosmic. We send our noble thoughts of peace to all corners of the universe, and we let noble thoughts of peace come to us from all the corners of the universe."

Mother had no watch, and nor did Gopalji. I could sense that Gopalji was ready to leave, yet somehow he felt that what he had said was inconclusive. He stood up, and so did Mother and I, but we did not move.

Gopalji looked serious, and he said: "But we mustn't think that personal peace is separate from world peace, nor world peace separate from cosmic peace. It is not that we have to wait for world peace until we have achieved personal peace. Personal, political, and planetary peace are to be pursued together. One includes and reinforces the others. One kind of peace is not possible without the others. The three dimensions of peace belong together." Gopalji smiled. Now he looked relaxed and with both palms together he bowed. Mother bowed to him and I touched his feet. He put his hand on my head in blessing.

Chapter 3

Mother Principle

GOPALJI HAD ENJOYED his *yogi chai* the previous day. He felt better; his sinuses had cleared a bit. He wanted more of the same. So after school he said, "I'll walk back with you and see if your mother will make me another cup of the spiced drink *ukali*."

Mother was pleased to know that her concoction was working, and was more than happy to offer him another dose. A herbal drink is always conducive to conversation.

"You know you spoke about Uma the other day. Wasn't she the consort of Shiva?" Mother asked.

"Yes she was, and no, she was not. There are thousands of myths about Mother Uma. All myths are a way to understand the world. Myths emerge from imagination. They elucidate an aspect of reality which goes beyond factual knowledge."

"What is your story of Uma, then?"

"Uma is the great Mother. She gave birth to all existence. She gives and will continue to give birth to the world. From Uma came Shiva. Then Uma and Shiva danced. So the world is the dance of Uma and Shiva; an unending dance, an everlasting dance."

When Gopalji stopped, Mother said,

"In our Jain tradition we are told that world is without beginning and without end."

"Yes, that is also true. We are not talking here about a linear concept of time. Uma and Shiva are always here, in continuous dance. All our movements, physical or mental, are part of that dance. Uma and Shiva are part of one body, half *devi* and half *deva*—half female, half male, half mother, half father. When half of Uma and half of Shiva became one body, the other half of Uma became all the feminine beings in the world, and the other half of Shiva became all the masculine beings in the world. I am talking in the past tense but it is also the present and the future. Time is fragmented only in language, not in reality.

"Uma is also Durga, the divine Mother riding on a lion, with eight arms, exerting her commanding power to defend life, protect the elements, and secure the continuity of the cosmic dance.

"Uma is also mother Saraswati, the benevolent and beautiful. She is gloriously riding a swan and playing music on the nine-stringed vina. Saraswati gives birth to imagination, poetry, music, arts, crafts, and the creativity of people and nature. The glowing shawls which you make with your hands and heart are the works of Saraswati active within you. Saraswati is manifesting through you. She nourishes all that one could imagine to produce beauty."

Gopalji's cold was no obstacle to his speaking. He stopped to cough and blow his nose; he was in no hurry to go home. Having sipped the yogi chai and moistened his throat, he continued: "Uma is also Mother Lakshmi, standing on the lotus flower, guarded by two elephants. She gives us all the beautiful gifts. The food for life flows from her mere presence. She is the mother of abundance. The melons and sesame growing on your farm, the fruit and honey on your trees, the milk and butter from your cows, are all granted by Mother Lakshmi. She is the goddess of wealth.

"But don't get carried away by the beauty and benevolence of Mother Uma. She is also the terrifying Kali. She brings an end to what has begun. She brings death to what is born, she wears a garland of skulls and holds a cup of blood. The lotus in her hand has a snake encircling it. Her sword and scissors cut through all and everything. Shiva himself is defeated by her and lies under her feet, his body surrounded by burning flames of fire.

"All that we see and cannot see, the entire existence, is held by Mother Uma. We are all in her embrace, in her lap, under her care. Trust Uma, trust the process of the unfolding universe. Just join the dance."

IT IS FASCINATING to me that Mother, a devout Jain, and Gopalji, a Hindu scholar, had such rapport with each other. Fascinating but not surprising. Jains have no notion of absolute truth. It is a philosophy of paradox: we are both spiritual and physical—"it is possible 'to be *and* not to be' "[1] at the same time. Everything is permanent and impermanent simultaneously:

"The language of the Jains is abstract," said Gopalji, continuing the conversation. "You call the process of the universe 'origination, cessation and persistence', in other words, birth, death and life; whereas the language of Hindus is pictorial and vivid. We have the trinity of Brahma the creator, Shiva the destroyer and Vishnu the maintainer. These three principles are presented by the Hindus in images, stories and myths. The Jains and the Hindus express the same underlying reality in different forms.

"Even though the three states of reality are named separately, they are not distinct. In every moment there is a Brahma, a Shiva and a Vishnu. They cannot be divided. There is no dualism. It is only in order to make sense of the world that we develop these three apparently separate Gods, but in the totality of existence they belong together."

Gopalji then explained himself with an example. "When a baby is born it is the work of Brahma. Then Vishnu takes over and maintains the life of the person. Then Shiva comes into play and brings an end to the life of that person as we knew it. But, on a subtle level, the birth of a baby is the death of the foetus, and thus Shiva performs his action first. As the baby is already an hour old, Shiva continues his drama of decay while allowing Vishnu to maintain the life of the baby. Of course Brahma is always present to keep renewing the cells and the soul of the baby. The three Gods are hard at work to hold the child's dynamic existence. Throughout life that person is dying every moment and also moving towards the final death, so Shiva is never at rest. And what we see as death must be the beginning of new life; the death of a tree is the birth of myriad lives in the soil."

The Hindu conviction of non-dualism also parallels the Jain view of non-absolutism. Sometimes non-dualism has been understood as a single reality. But Gopalji believed that "non-dualism represents the multifaceted nature of the cosmos, rather than 'one' or the 'other'. Multiplicity is not fragmentation or disconnection, it is an interrelated whole which can never be entirely captured in words. When one speaks, one can only speak of a particular aspect of truth, never the whole truth. Hence we should recognise that we may never be in full possession of total and absolute understanding, at least not in language, or in the mind. Language can only approximate a particular aspect of truth. And beyond that, one can only remain silent.

"For example, there is water in a pond, there is water in a well, there is water in a river and in the ocean. Even the snow is water. These waters are particular expressions of the same element. Water manifests in many forms, and a particular manifestation has particular relevance according to climatic and geographic conditions. There is no contradiction between the universal water and the multiple, particular waters. Thus, rather than *the* Water, there are waters. Similarly, rather than *the* truth, there are truths. Rather than *the* religion, there are religions.

"A frog in a pond who has never seen the sea may dispute with a fish that there is any such thing as the sea, and say that the only water is the water in the pond. A frog may even, in its preference for a particular pond, ridicule another pond. This is because of a fragmented view. In the eyes of the wise there is no fundamental difference between these various waters. Why waste time in disputation, one truth against another truth, or one religion against another religion? Why not open the third eye and see multi-faceted reality?"

One of the meditation techniques practised by Gopalji was to focus between the eyebrows just above the bridge of the nose, which is the symbolic place of the third eye. "Close your two eyes and allow the third eye to open," he said. "The third eye helps to transcend the dualism of the differentiating two eyes. The third eye lets in an *impressionistic* picture of the world—where the inner and outer worlds meld and merge. The third eye sees the connections, the relationships, the patterns, the mutuality.

"The two eyes see three-dimensional reality—the gross and the obvious. But to see non-dimensional reality we require the Third Eye—the eye of the imagination, the eye of intuition, the eye of the spirit. The third eye perceives unlimited reality, the eternal, the infinite, the whole, the complete. It has a translucent quality, which enlightens us beyond mental formations and intellectual conclusions. The third eye is the eye of love—all-seeing, all-accepting, all-receiving and yet clinging to nothing, owning nothing, holding nothing, rejecting nothing, having nothing."

In conclusion, Gopalji said, "There is no *one* Truth." Affirming Gopalji's views, Mother added, "The Jains call this '*anekant*', which means 'no absolute knowledge, no final answer'. There is no exclusive formation of truth. In the Jain tradition there is a phrase, 'this is true and that is also true'. There are truths, and they are always contextual; a text can only have meaning in its context. Truth is sublime. Truth is not a 'correct' belief system. It is not a point of arrival: it is a continuous process, a continuous search and a continuous way of being. A seeker of truth can have no fixed position; there is no dogma. As the mind expands, truth expands. Therefore Jains attempt to live without trampling on another's life or thoughts, and practise generosity of the spirit."

Mother went further, and said, "Truth is elusive. We should not impose our truth on others. This spirit of non-imposition is non-violence, and so non-violence is a prerequisite for truth.

"The world is a mystery, knowledge is limited, life is a journey of constant discoveries. One need not fear uncertainty and unpredictability. What we know is relative and constrained by the facts available to us at any given time. When we discover new facts we need to discover ourselves in a fresh manner. This is the way to keep our knowledge renewed."

For the Jains, all knowledge is provisional, conditional and hypothetical. This theory of probability is called *syadvada*. Whatever we know needs to be qualified by a 'perhaps' or a 'maybe'. "We cannot affirm or deny anything absolutely. There is nothing certain on account of the endless complexity of things."[2] Whatever we speak, we speak from a certain point of view. Therefore all formulations and expressions are provisional points of view.

Mother told us a traditional story. Once there were six blind men, and one day they heard that the local prince had acquired a new elephant. The blind men had heard of elephants. but they had never met one. So they decided to go to the palace of the prince and find out what an elephant was. When they reached the palace, the guard let the six men in. The first man touched the elephant's side, the second touched the trunk, the third felt the tusk, the fourth man the leg, the fifth the ear, and the sixth the tail. Then they rested under a tree and began to talk about their experiences.

"Now I know the elephant is like a wall," said the first man, who had touched its sides.

"Oh no! It is like a snake," replied the second man, who had touched the trunk.

"You both must be stupid," objected the third, who had touched the tusks. "The elephant is like a spear."

"Have you gone mad? The elephant is like a tree," cried the fourth man, who had touched the leg.

"You are all wrong. The elephant is like a fan," said the fifth man, who had touched the ears.

"No, no, it is like a rope," yelled the sixth man, who had felt the tail. A huge row ensued. They were about to come to blows when the prince came to ride the elephant. He asked, "Why are you all so agitated?"

"We cannot agree on what an elephant is like," said one of the blind men. "We all touched the same animal, but to each of us the animal was completely different."

The prince laughed. "The elephant is a large animal; its side is like a wall, trunk like a snake, with tusks like spears, legs like tree trunks, ears like fans and a tail like a rope. You have to put all those aspects together, then it is the whole elephant."

This story reveals that all knowledge is partial. Realising this, we can be free of fixed ideas and opinions. Free of fundamentalism. We can accept plurality of beliefs and yet be free of beliefs.

Rise to the complete and holistic view. Look at the world and see it whole with all the wealth of its attributes. "Always be open to learn and to discover," Mother said.

"That is a lovely story—six blind men discovering an elephant!" said Gopalji. The evening was drawing in. As Mother reached for an oil lamp, Gopalji said, "My family awaits me at home; I must go."

* * *

Chapter 4

The Joy of Making

IN OUR HOUSE there were no books, no newspapers, no magazines, no radio, no television, and of course no computers. Our lives were filled with conversations. They were deep, intimate, informal and easy. But the pressure to be literate was entering our family. Father was literate. He could keep his accounts and write letters. My three brothers were the same. My four sisters never learned to read or write. But Gopalji had persuaded Mother to let me go to him at least a few hours a day, so that I was not left out of the literate world. Mother respected Gopalji, and trusted him. He had a small, one-class school, whose numbers fluctuated between ten and twenty. In addition to the time spent on reading and writing, we learned Sanskrit and Hindi verses by heart.

"You can only depend on the knowledge in your head and the money in your pocket," he used to say. He taught us basic maths, reading and writing. No history, no geography, no arts nor sports. "You should learn all that at home," he would say. But he would tell us ancient stories—the great Hindu myths as related in the Ramayana and Mahabharata, epic poems of war and peace. His school was not intended to replace home. Home was the first and foremost school, and our parents were the first and foremost teachers. Gopalji's class was only a supplement.

THIS WAS FINE for me. I enjoyed the company of my mother, and I enjoyed watching her making things by hand. In between milking, making butter, cooking, walking to the fields and philosophising, Mother found half an hour here, an hour there, to lay colourful patterns on cloth. She made shawls, skirts and bedspreads. Quite often she used pieces of old cloth and put them together as a patchwork, on which she would embroider using pieces of mirror. She considered such craftwork important and integral to her life.

One day Mother gave a recently completed shawl to my sister Suraj as a present. Suraj was delighted.

"It is a lovely shawl, Mother—so soft, so vivid. I am going to put it in a prominent place on the wall for everyone to see. I am not going to spoil it by wearing it. I might spill something on it, which would be a great shame."

Mother was not pleased with such exuberant enthusiasm for displaying her shawl on the wall. For her, art and craft were not for decoration or exhibition, but for use.

"I have made it for you to wear. It is not for show. When you start to put beautiful things on the walls, you start to put ugly things on your bodies. So wear it, wear it! Learn to make beautiful and useful things, which are durable, so that when the old ones begin to decay, new ones are ready."

'Beautiful, useful, durable'; the words stuck, and ever since have reverberated in my mind. The walls of our house were bare, but everything we used—pots, beds, tools, shoes, and other objects of daily life—were well made and beautiful. Beauty was intrinsic.

"Mother, you do such lovely needlework, but it takes you so long to make a single piece—sometimes six months, sometimes a year or even longer. These days you can get clever sewing machines which can perform the same work in a fraction of the time. May I get you one?" sister Suraj suggested.

"Why?" Mother asked

"It will save you time, Mother."

"Is there a shortage of time? Have you not heard of eternity, my dear, eternity? When the Gods made time, they made plenty of it. I have no shortage of time. For me time is not running out, time is always coming. There is always tomorrow, next week, next month, next year—even next life, so what is the hurry?" Suraj did not seem convinced. "Isn't it better to save time and save labour so that we can do other things, and more of them?"

"You are trying to save something which is infinite, and expend things which are finite. A sewing machine is made of metal, and there is only a limited amount of metal in the world. Also you have to mine to get the metal. You have to have factories to make machines, so you need even more finite materials to build these factories. So much violence in mining, so much violence in factories! How many creatures get killed, how many human beings have to suffer doing such tasks like going deep underground to mine the metal? I have heard about their suffering. Why should we make them suffer for our convenience?" Suraj seemed to understand.

Encouraged by her nodding, Mother continued. "Whereas my physical energy is not in short supply, it is always there. I enjoy the work, too. For me it is meditation. Meditation is not just chanting mantras or sitting quietly in the lotus position and counting the breath. Sewing, cooking, washing, cleaning, every activity done with a sense of the sacred is meditation. Do you want to take away my meditation? When I am busy with my needle I am peaceful, everything is so silent, so calm. Your machine will make so much noise, which will disturb me. I can't imagine myself being able to meditate when the machine is going clickety-clack, clickety-clack.

"Besides, this might be only a mirage of the mind that a machine will make me work less. I might end up making ten shawls per year instead of one or two, and use even more materials. Even if I saved time, what would I do with it? I treasure the joy of work."

This was absolutely true; Mother seemed to be in bliss when she was embroidering. No two pieces of work were ever the same. She took pleasure in inventing new patterns and designs. Of course she never thought in advance what pattern she would produce: she improvised her design as she went along. The most striking part of Mother's needlework was the amount of pleasure and happiness she drew from it.

"I tell you, children, I don't make shawls for anything other than to make shawls, because this is my joy, my *ananda*. This is why Hindu sadhus include the word 'ananda' in their name. Yogananda, for example—it is no good to have only yoga without joy, without ananda. One can be ascetic. Go and live in a cave. Stand on one's head for hours. Yoga in the morning, in the afternoon, in the evening, yoga every day, but no joy. Such yoga becomes a burden, an obsession. That is why a true yogi is always called Yogananda. Yoga alone is not enough: it is the joy in yoga which makes yoga a way of good life.

"Other *sadhus* are called Satyananda—joy in truth, Vivekananda—joy in wisdom, Atmananda—joyful soul, Shivananda—joy in the company of Shiva and so on."

Suraj and I were listening attentively. "But there is also sorrow in our lives. We cannot always be in the ecstasy of ananda, or can we?" asked Suraj, "For example, when Father died you were very sad; you cried for days, I remember. Everybody was sad. How can you have joy when you are engulfed in the sea of such sadness and loss?"

The expression on Mother's face suddenly changed—remembering Father's death was painful, and her feelings were still very sore. It took her a few moments to collect herself and be able to speak to us. She reached for her sewing kit and started to engage in a piece of work which was still being made. She needed this meditative distraction. Then she said, "Yes there is sorrow, yes there is pain; we all have to suffer. Birth is pain, sickness is pain, death is pain. When someone is disagreeable to you, that hurts. That is why the thought of joy, of ananda, is so necessary and helpful. We can make the sorrow and suffering into a compost out of which the roses of joy can grow. This is a continuous quest, and we have to keep sowing the rose seeds and not just get overwhelmed by compost.

"A lotus is rooted in the deep mud of the pond, and yet the flower itself is so soft, so beautiful, so serene. The petals have a subtle oily quality so that any water from the pond or rain pouring over it rolls away—the lotus is never damaged or drowned. That is why the lotus is a sacred flower, a spiritual symbol of joy. The lotus is our guru, our teacher. It shows us a way to accept sorrow and serenity simultaneously.

"The duck always lives on the lake, cold or warm, day or night, asleep or awake. It also has an oily quality in its feathers. Water is so powerful, so overwhelming, yet the duck swims right through it, and water just rolls off its back. So we can learn from the duck how to swim in the sea of sorrow and remain joyful."

Then Mother came to the point:

"Yes, your father's death left a great hole in my life, in the lives of everybody in the family, and in the lives of his friends. But our friend Gopalji reminds us that the soul never dies. As we change our old clothes for new clothes, the soul leaves the old body behind to take on a new body. So from the point of view of your father, death was liberating and freeing. We need to see death not in negative terms, not as an end of life but as a door to new life. If there were no death, we would be stuck here for ever. It is birth which causes more problems than death. Once you are born you have to go through the valley of life, encountering disappointment, disputes and depression; experiencing anger, anxiety, craving, and attachment. So birth is to be blamed for the sorrows of life, not death. Wouldn't it be nice if our individual soul became part of the universal soul and remained there?"

This was a staggering question for me. Ever since Father's death I had been wondering, "How can we be free of death so that no one has to cry, so that my Mother doesn't have to be lonely, so that I and children like me are never without their fathers?" I had been thinking that I would do anything, go anywhere, endure all difficulties, to bring an end to death. Now Mother was saying that to bring an end to death is to bring an end to birth. How puzzling, how perplexing.

We can't help that we are born. Now we have to travel through the valley of life. Yet Mother seemed to have found a nice footpath, a path of joy.

"I am not always in joy. I drift from it and return to it. Every year a snake leaves its old skin behind and moves swiftly away from it. In the same way, the nature of life is such that we develop a skin of attachments, expectations, ambitions, so we need to do what a snake does, keep leaving this skin behind so that our soul can touch the ground of joy, ananda. As long as we are in this body, in this world, and in the net of relationships, we are bound to collect unwholesome baggage. Ananda can free us from this baggage."

Chapter 5

Going to Ladnun: Meeting the Guru

AT LEAST ONCE a year Mother would go to visit our *gurudev*, Tulsi, the head of our Jain order. This is called *darshan*, which means a sacred glimpse of a holy person or image in a temple. On one occasion our guru was in Ladnun, a medieval town some fifty miles from our home. Early in the morning my mother and I took the narrow-gauge train pulled by a steam engine. It couldn't have been going at much more than ten or fifteen miles per hour. We settled down in the train as if it was going to be our home for a while. Mother had packed many delicious snacks to ease the journey: sweet crumble balls made with flour, butter and sugar, almond cakes and *parathas*, flat breads fried in butter, together with various dips and chutneys. We shared the food with our fellow travellers, who shared their dishes with us. By the time we arrived in Ladnun it was late afternoon.

We stayed in the guest house of our Oswal community. Oswals are Jain merchants. In many towns the Oswals have built guest houses where visitors can stay, free of charge. These houses are also used for weddings, funerals, festivals, and any other communal functions or gatherings. While they provided pots, pans, bedding, rugs, floor mats and canopies, we brought our own foodstuffs—rice, lentils, beans, peas, oil, salt, spices, sweets and sun-dried vegetables. This guest house was exclusively for the Oswal community; various other castes and sub-castes have their own guest houses. Some of them even provide free meals to their visitors. There were no hotels in this town of 100,000 people. So these free guest houses were a way for each community to take care of their visitors on a manageable scale, and on the basis of hospitality. The Oswal guest house was built with donations from the Oswal community of Ladnun. We were not required to make any payment, but it was expected that we would provide similar hospitality to visiting guests in our own town.

Mother and I enjoyed walking about in Ladnun. The traditional houses, called *havellis*, were large, with enormous wooden doors which were opened only when horses or elephants or camels needed to pass through; otherwise there was a small door within the large gate for people to enter. These gates were great both in size and in workmanship. The panels were densely studded with brass knobs, giving a glow. Beside the gates on the walls were frescos of elephants and horses, painted in vivid blue, red and yellow. At the top of these gates would be the elephant-headed Hindu deity, Ganesh, the son of Lord Shiva, who brings grace and good fortune to householders, prevents any evil spirit entering the house and bestows blessing on those who enter the house with good intentions. Many of the Jain families were happy to put the fresco of Ganesh above their doors.

"It was Ganesh who was the scribe of poet Vyasa, and wrote down word for word the entire epic of the Mahabharata," Mother explained. "There was no one else who could keep up with the fluency and flow of Vyasa's poem; only Ganesh could do it. But the problem was that Ganesh was almost too fast a scribe. Ganesh said to Vyasa, 'Yes, I will offer my services. I am at your disposal, please use me, but on one condition: once I start writing I cannot stop. So you have to dictate your poem without a pause.'

"This worried Vyasa. He could not write the epic without Ganesh, but could he keep up with Ganesh? Quickly and cleverly, Vyasa thought of a way round the problem. He said 'Yes, I accept your condition; but I too have one condition, you must not write down anything until you have understood it. You are not to write down mechanically what I say. You have to take it in, you have to understand and enjoy the story.' In this way, when Vyasa needed time to think ahead he made up some complex verses which Ganesh had to ponder over to understand, and this gave Vyasa sufficient pause. Ganesh surrendered to this command, and thus the Mahabharata was composed."

"But how did he get this elephant's head, Mother?" I asked.

"Oh, there are many different stories about that. One explanation is that Shiva, the father, wanted a son who was half man and half animal to unite the two worlds. Shiva chose the elephant because it is the wisest of all animals, and so Ganesh is the embodiment of elephant wisdom.

"But there is also another story:

"After Goddess Uma (also known as Parvati) had married Shiva and had conceived Ganesh, she sent Shiva to find a beautiful place in the plains where she could make a home to bring up their family. It took many years for Shiva to find such a place. In the end he found it: it was Varanasi, on the banks of the river Ganges. Having put his trident in the ground to mark the place, he returned to Mount Kailash in the Himalayas to announce the good news of his find.

"When he arrived back, he saw a young man guarding the path. Shiva demanded that the young man get out of his way so that he could reach

Uma. But the young man refused, saying that he was guarding Uma and no one was allowed to pass. 'How dare you stand between Uma and me!' Shiva was suspicious, jealous and outraged. He thought, 'Who is this young man, what is he doing here?' A battle ensued. Shiva, the god of death, cut off the young man's head.

"Hearing the commotion, Uma rushed to the scene and was horrified. She cried 'What have you done? You have killed our son!'

"Shiva, realising his folly, begged Uma, 'Tell me what can I do now, how can I restore life to my son?'

"Uma said, 'Go quickly and take the head of the first living being you meet, and place it on our son's body.' Shiva went searching, and the first creature he met was an elephant. He took the elephant's head and placed it on his son's shoulders, and thus it was that Ganesh got an elephant head!"

To me it seemed a strange story. How could a god be so stupid as to kill his own son, and still be considered a god? But then I was too young to understand the deep meanings of myths.

IN LADNUN, THE houses belonging to the wealthy were built with a local stone and intricately carved. There were elaborate stone screens, designed to let fresh air and light enter, without bringing too much of the sun's heat. Those beautiful screens had a useful function. But while the masons were at work, they carved peacocks, swans, horses, elephants, tigers, trees, lotuses and many other forms in the screens. Mother and I were intrigued and amazed to see house after house carved and painted with such elegance. These havellis are well known as examples of traditional buildings. We entered one of them to see the splendour of the architecture. Immediately inside the great doorway there were two rooms, one on each side, mostly used by the men of the family and their male visitors. Then there was a spacious unpaved courtyard in which was standing an old *neem* tree.

"Neem is the most medicinal tree in the world. It is antiseptic, healing and purifying. That is why most people have at least one neem in their courtyard," Mother commented. The courtyard was being used to dry vegetables and store firewood, and there were stables for horses and camels. One corner of this large courtyard was the main house, which was itself built around an inner courtyard, paved with stone, where the women and children lived, where food was cooked and water stored. Mother and I ventured in, and the family inside was most welcoming. Mother explained that we had come from some distance in order to receive religious teachings from our gurudev, Tulsi. "But since it is my son's first visit to Ladnun, I am showing him around."

One member of the family, a woman probably in her early twenties, offered us cool, refreshing water. The inner courtyard had a veranda running round the edges, from which hung heavy curtains to protect the rooms from sand, dust and the scorching heat of the sun.

I was highly excited to be walking around Ladnun and encountering these huge havellis shading the narrow lanes. There were women wearing saris of many bright colours, some threaded with gold or silver, with gorgeous jewellery—toe rings, ankle bracelets, bangles, rings, upper arm bands, necklaces, earrings, nose rings—almost every part of the body seemed to have some ornament on it. The men were not far behind either: they wore colourful turbans, earrings and necklaces. Obviously Ladnun was a rich and elegant town. Many residents went far away to big cities like Kolkata (Calcutta), earned their fortune, and spent it in their home town, building opulent havellis.

* * *

Chapter 6

A Jain View of Reality

*"Just as a mighty mango tree is hidden within the stone of the mango,
so is divinity itself hidden within you. Rest not until you uncover it."*
—Bhagwan Mahavir

OUR FIRST AFTERNOON and evening were mostly spent walking around
Ladnun and settling down in the guest house. The next day, we awoke
around sunrise and went to have *darshan*, the 'holy glimpse' of the guru.

For every Jain devotee it is an essential practice to begin the day with
the darshan of a holy person or sacred image in a temple. It must be done
before breakfast, before work, before any form of activity, so that the spirit
of the encounter can permeate the day and every activity. A spiritual person or a sacred image is a medium through which one can see purity, spirituality, beauty and unity in all beings and in all things.

While giving his blessings, guru Tulsi said, "May all beings upon this
Earth be happy, fulfilled and self-realised. May they be free from all afflic-
tions and liberated from bondage."

Hundreds of men, women and children gathered in their devotion to
receive darshan and blessings. The whole ritual lasted about five to ten
minutes, and there was a profound sense of devotion in the air.

Later, Mother and I were present at a teaching session, where gurudev
Tulsi elucidated Jain philosophy. He was using the Sanskrit text of
Tattvartha Sutra, written by Umasvati, a second century Jain philosopher
and monk. His theme was the seven strands of reality, 'that which is'—
tattva. To discuss this he began with an analogy.

"Take the example of a house. Before the house is built there is empty,
clear space. This is the universal space; this is the first reality of the life
force, *jiva*. Then we build four walls to give a form to that space; this form
is the physical body, called *ajiva*. The house has doors and windows through
which air, water, wood, dust, food, furniture, clothes and umpteen other
objects are brought in. Similarly the human body has an inflow through the

five senses, which is called *asrava*. The time comes when the house is cluttered with too many material possessions. The inhabitants of the house start to feel oppressed and burdened by the liking of some goods and the dislike of others; this is bondage (*bandha*). So the inhabitants decide to stop any new thing from coming into the house. They close the doors, shut the windows, and block all the holes, even the openings through which rain or air may enter; this is psychological and spiritual defence (*samvara*). Then the householders realise that even this is not enough, they want to be free of the possessions they have already accumulated. So one by one they put their possessions on a fire and start to free themselves from all burdens; this is called purification (*nirjara*). Then the householders feel, Why should we be attached to this particular house? Why have ownership of anything at all? Why be bound and controlled, and have our lives dictated by this house? So they get rid of the house itself, and then that universal space which had been turned into an enclosed individual space becomes a universal space again—space has been liberated. This is the state of free spirit, inner liberation, enlightenment (*moksha*)."

THEN GURUDEV went into a detailed and precise explanation of the seven states of existence, most of which went straight over my head at that time, but later I became quite familiar with these concepts. These seven states of reality can be summarised as follows.

The first is life force (jiva). It is also known as the atman, soul, self, spirit, energy, void, anima, consciousness, mind, emptiness, formlessness, subjectivity, the being in its metaphysical aspect. Life pervades everything. From a blade of grass and a dewdrop to Himalayan mountains, everything has life, not just humans and animals, but all elements are living.

The second is matter (ajiva). We see it as body, form, structure, shape, solidity and objects. Everything, all phenomena and elements—earth, air, fire, water, plants, humans, animals, are made of these two essentials. Jiva, the unmanifest life force, manifests through ajiva, matter. Matter embodies soul.

We cannot know life (jiva), without matter (ajiva). Life permeates matter, matter holds life. They are in an intricate dance of existence. The tree-ness of a tree, the mango-ness of a mango, the humanity of a human being, are Jiva. The inner is Jiva and the outer is Ajiva. Jiva is quality, continuity and permanence. Ajiva is quantity, change and impermanence. Jiva and Ajiva together shape the world and cause all things to exist.

The third is the inflow and outflow through the senses (asrava). It is the process by which life (jiva) connects and relates to material and sensory objects. It is the ability to feel, think, act, reflect, judge, remember and perform every other conceivable action. Through the senses come thoughts and actions, and from these comes the inflow of forces which have positive or negative influence on all beings.

The fourth is bondage (bandha). This means that life gets bound in likes and dislikes, attraction and repulsion, attachment and aversion, pain and pleasure, all pairs of opposites. It gets conditioned and bound by desirable or undesirable consequences, which resulted from the influx. These inflows create conditioning and are called *karmas*. They have a glue-like quality, making them stick on to a living being (jiva). Through bondage we suffer, we are held back from liberation.

The fifth is defence (samvara). This is the first step towards liberation and the cessation of suffering. A living being (jiva) recognises the suffering caused by bondage and chooses to stop the inflow of forces which create craving, clinging, revulsion and delusion. So all the openings and channels which allow the inflow of karma, which corrupt the soul, are blocked. All attachments are renounced and a path of restraint is followed by the person practising samvara.

The sixth is purification (nirjara). It cleans all the conditioning and karmas which have been gathered in the past. Once the inflow of good and bad forces is stopped, then the person pursues the path of clearing out the clutter accumulated within. This is a kind of bonfire to burn all karma, all conditioning, all prejudices and all bondage. Purification (nirjara) is like water, washing away the dirt of karma. This is done through penance, austerity, service and sacrifice. As a result a state of equilibrium is achieved. The soul is now clean, constant, unwavering, unperturbed and unagitated. Now one is able to witness the drama of the world without getting drawn into it.

Finally comes liberation (moksha). This is the state of enlightenment (*nirvana*), total inner freedom (*mukti*). At this stage a living being accomplishes self-realisation, which is to be integrated with the universal soul, *anima mundi* (atman becomes paramatman). In this liberated state there is no subject or object, there is no birth nor death, there is no fragmentation. It is a state of wholeness, completeness and totality.

THE GURUDEV TULSI had finished the morning's discourse. The disciples kneeled and bowed to him. We placed our palms together, one hand representing the guru, the other hand the disciples, brought together in union.

Mother and I returned to the guest house. We sorted our belongings—we had five pieces of luggage: two bedrolls, one small metal trunk for our clothes, one hessian bag full of rice, lentils, wheat flour, spices, oil, ghee, etc. And the other bag contained pots, pans, a wooden board, a rolling pin, and so on.

After creating a bit of order, I helped Mother cook the meal, and then we waited to see if any monks would pass by with begging bowls so that we could share our food with them. We did not have to wait too long. An older monk in his late fifties came. He had three begging bowls stacked on top of each other, which he carried in a cloth. We urged him to take some food from us, which he did. Mother placed rice and bread (*chapati*) in one bowl, some cooked vegetables in another, and lentil soup (*dhal*) in the third. Mother wanted to give more but the monk took only a little. He collected food from many families, which he would share with other monks.

After our lunch we sat together reciting mantras, and singing devotional songs which Mother knew by heart and I was learning.

We were eagerly waiting to hear more of gurudev's teaching. He had announced that he would be speaking about the meaning of karma. He had used this word a number of times in today's session and everyone was keen to learn more. Mother was determined not to miss any of his sessions. So the next morning Mother and I were among the first to arrive. Gurudev started to talk about the nature of karma and its cause.

"Every action contains reaction," gurudev said. "There is nothing we can do which is without repercussions. Every word we utter, every thought we think, every desire we feel, will have a consequence, an effect, on ourselves as well as on others. Every seed we sow produces fruits, and each fruit contains further seed, and that seed will again bear fruit. This is the law of karma. If you speak sweet words to someone, you will get a sweet response in return. If you insult someone, you will receive abuses in return. Even if you do not receive any abuse, you will suffer from your own inner turbulence and agitation. Anger has an immediate effect on your emotional state. This kind of instant cause and effect is easy to see, but karma includes the long-term—very long-term—relationship between an action and its consequence. Every life (jiva) is a repository where all the residue of the slightest thought to the greatest action is preserved; even if it is not present in the conscious memory, it stays there in the unconscious (*samskara*), like possessions forgotten in the attic. We cannot predict when they will emerge, and when they do, the action they cause will contain the seeds of further karma. Thus karma is subtle matter which sticks, lingers, conditions, hangs around and bothers the soul. Karma keeps life bound with positive and negative strings (*punya* and *papa*)."

This sounded as if we are caught in the cycle of actions and reactions for ever and ever. "Is there a way out of this karmic maze?" a disciple asked.

Tulsi answered, "Yes there is. It is living in compassion, *dharma*. As karma captures, binds and holds our physical and mental interactions, dharma liberates us from all conditioning and all trappings. Dharma is the spiritual sustenance, and is the antidote to karma.

"The word comes from the root 'dhar' meaning holding, keeping, preserving, maintaining, supporting, observing, remembering. The word 'dharaa' or 'dharani', which means the earth, comes from the same root. Dharma, like the earth, sustains all life.

"What destroys is violence (himsa), the source of karma. What maintains is non-violence (ahimsa), the supreme dharma. We need to learn to practise non-violence, meaning not violating the dignity and sanctity of the Other. When we violate others, we violate ourselves, because others are us. We are all related. We are all made of the same stuff, the same earth, air, fire, water, space, time and consciousness. These same elements take different forms. They appear in one form, then are transformed into another. Ultimately there is neither I nor mine, the universe belongs to itself. We are all part of Life.

"By living a life of compassion (dharma) we prevent the inflow of karma. We need not engage in any action in order to live in accordance with dharma. We only need to restrain from damaging action. Dharma is to be good rather than do good. This journey from doing to being is a sublime journey, a subtle journey. While just being we do not accumulate karma. In fact, we are more truly ourselves when we are in the mode of being rather than doing. In dharma, action happens without doing. The sun does not move, and yet it radiates light. Non-doing does not mean non-action. Being your own nature is dharma, like water always stays as water, and by being water, quenches thirst and cleans dirt. Goodness simply flows out of Being. Karma is striving, dharma is effortless. Karma is contrived, dharma is natural. Desire, ambition and goals are part of Karma. Karma causes success or disappointment. Action performed without desire is dharma. Dharma is appreciation of what is. Dharma is to be at rest, at peace, contented and natural. Karma causes suffering and dharma is the way to end suffering. Karma wounds; dharma heals. Karma causes anguish and distress, for which dharma is the therapy."

After a short reflective pause, gurudev Tulsi said,

"In Buddhist teachings there are four Noble Truths. 1. Suffering, or dukkha, which is equivalent to the Jain principle of bondage or bandha. 2. Causes of suffering, which compares with the Jain notion of sentience or asrava. 3. Cessation of suffering; this is similar to our concept of defence or samvara. 4. Paths to end suffering, or marga. This is close to our practice of purification or nirjara.

"The Buddhists also accept the state of enlightenment or total liberation. They call it nirvana, Jains call it moksha, but the meaning is the same.

"However, the Buddhists don't discuss the existence of soul or the life force (jiva). But the Jains say, 'suffering, yes. But who suffers? Who feels pain? Who follows the path to end pain? Who is enlightened?' The Buddhists do not answer these questions. They say that these are irrelevant or unnecessary speculations. But for the Jains, jiva (life force) is part of the elementary existence. It is jiva which suffers from delusions, and it is jiva which frees itself from those delusions.

"Having said all that, this is not a dogmatic position. From one point of view there is jiva or life force which transcends matter, but from another point of view, there is no self, like an object. Even the Buddhists may agree that there is life force, whatever the name."

Having reconciled the Buddhist and Jain positions, gurudev Tulsi seemed happy. This generosity of spirit is very much part of Jain 'inclusivity' (anekant).

The discourse was over. We bowed in gratitude, and gurudev raised his right hand in blessing.

MOTHER HAD A PLAN for the afternoon. "Our order of Jains is not the only Jain community in Ladnun," she said, and she took me to visit the Jain temple in the centre of town. It was exciting to be going to a temple because our gurudev was not in favour of image worship. There are two parallel Jain traditions: one advocates image worship as an essential path of devotion and object of meditation; the other recommends a practice which is free of any material forms such as temples, bells, statues, incense and candles. Our family belongs to the latter tradition. However, mother, being a free spirit, was always open to receive insights and wisdom from all traditions. In particular she wanted me to know about the existence of the temple tradition.

When we arrived at the temple the caretaker welcomed us, as he does all visitors who are not part of his community. "We need you to guide us," said Mother, so he took us around the hall, and pointing towards the sacred images he related the stories of the Jain masters of ancient times (the tirthankaras). Seeing Mother so deeply absorbed in the stories, the caretaker said, "There is another, much older temple under ground, under our feet. Would you like to see it?"

"Yes, yes," said Mother with great excitement.

The caretaker took a key from his pocket and opened a small door, with stone steps down to a subterranean temple. "The Jains built this temple," the caretaker explained, "at a time of persecution."

There were many beautiful images in red, black, green and white marble, but what intrigued me most was a small brass plate placed upright on a stand. In its centre the outline of a standing human figure was cut, representing the released spirit—the being who has attained total liberation (moksha). In this representation the figure has no solidity; the figure is the space. Its shape is only revealed by the brass around it. The figure itself is empty.

THE AWAITED MORNING SESSION with gurudev came once more. When we had all gathered, he began:

"Non-violence is common to all four great religions which originated in India: Hindu, Buddhist, Sikh and Jain. However, the Jains pay much greater attention to compassion for animals. Being a Jain is synonymous with being vegetarian.

"According to Jain scholars, there are 8.4 million living species upon the Earth. An inventory of all these species was prepared by the Jains over 2,000 years ago. It includes eagles, swans, whales, tigers, elephants, snakes, worms, bacteria, fungi, air, water, fire, rocks and everything which is natural and alive. Jains are animists—for them, everything natural is living, and all life is sacred. Any kind of harm to any form of life is to be avoided or minimised. Of course, the sustenance of one form of life depends upon the others, yet we should never take this for granted.

"Human beings are only one of those 8.4 million species. They have no more rights than any other species. All living beings, human and other-than-human, have an equal right to life. Not only do humans have no absolute rights—to take, to control, or to subjugate other forms of life—but they also have extra obligations to practise non-violence, and be humble in the face of the mysterious, glorious, abundant and extraordinary phenomenon of the living world."

Gurudev told us a story which exemplifies the Jain attitude towards animals.

"Once there was a young prince called Parshwanath, who at the time of his marriage was heading towards the house of his bride. He saw an enclosure of animals, tightly packed, waiting to be slaughtered. Shocked by the cry of the animals, the prince enquired, 'Why are those animals being kept in such cruel conditions?' His aides replied, 'They are for the feast of your wedding party.'

"The young prince was overwhelmed with compassion. Arriving at the wedding chamber, he spoke with the father of the princess, 'Immediately and unconditionally all those animals enclosed to be slaughtered for the marriage feast must be freed,' he said. 'Why?' asked her father. 'The lives of animals are there for the pleasures of humans. Animals are our slaves and our meat. How can there be any feast without the flesh?'

"Prince Parshwanath was puzzled. He could not believe what he had just heard. He exclaimed, 'Animals have souls, they have consciousness, they are our kith and kin, they are our ancestors. They wish to live as much as we do; they have feelings and emotions. They have love and passion; they fear death as much as we do. Their instinct for life is no less than ours. Their right to live is as fundamental as our own. I cannot marry, I cannot love, and I cannot enjoy life if animals are enslaved and killed.'

"Without further ado he rejected the plans for his marriage, walked out of the wedding chamber, discarded the comfortable life of a prince, and responded to his inner calling to go out and awaken the sleepy masses who had been conditioned to think selfishly and kill animals for their pleasure and comfort.

"The animal kingdom welcomed Parshwanath as the prophet of the weak and the wild. They gathered around him. The birds sat upon the trees nearby; fishes came to the corner of the lake where Parshwanath was seated. Elephants, lions, foxes, rabbits, rats, insects and ants paid homage to him. One day, finding Parshwanath being soaked by heavy monsoon rain, the king of the cobras stood on his tail and created an umbrella with his huge head." I remembered seeing the black marble statue of Parshwanath with the seven-headed cobra protecting him, at the Jain temple the previous day.

Gurudev continued, "Thousands upon thousands of people in villages, towns, and cities were moved by the teachings of Parshwanath. They renounced meat and took up the work of animal welfare. The princess whom Parshwanath was going to marry was so inspired that she decided to remain unmarried and dedicate herself to the care of animals. Having lost a daughter and would-be son-in-law to the cause of peace with animals, the King himself underwent transformation. He announced that all animals were to be respected in his kingdom, and that there would be no hunting, no shooting, no caging, and no pets.

"Parshwanath was the twenty-third Great Liberator (tirthankara) of animals and humans in the Jain tradition. The twenty-fourth was Mahavir, who lived 2,600 years ago. All the twenty-four Great Liberators have an animal associated with them, symbolising that in Jain teachings the place of animals is central. Love is not love if it does not include love of animals. What kind of compassion is it which adores human life, but ignores the slaughter of animals?

"Division between humans and animals and putting human interests before animal interests is the beginning of sectionalism, racism, nationalism, class and caste discrimination, and of course speciesism. The same mindset, which enslaves animals, goes on to enslave humans in the name of self-interest, national interest, and umpteen other narrow interests. Therefore we, the Jains, advocate an unconditional and unequivocal reverence for all life."

Chapter 7

Dharma Practice

"YOUR FATHER SHOULD have been with us today." Totally unexpectedly, Mother was overcome with emotion. Tears rolled down her cheeks. This was not an unusual occurrence. Father's death had left her continuously grieving. Seeing Mother in such a state made me very unhappy. There must be many mothers like mine whose husbands had died and left them grieving. There must be many children like me who were growing up without their fathers, I thought. Is there a way of stopping this demon of death swallowing people in such a merciless way?, I wondered.

"Why did Father die?" I asked.

"What do you mean, 'why'? All those who are born will die one day. I will die, and my son, you too will die." Mother spoke with a firm voice, and yet she was unable to come to terms with Father's death.

While Mother was preparing lunch I quietly sneaked out. I went back to gurudev Tulsi. Fortunately for me, he was not surrounded by his usual followers; only two or three young monks were sitting by him. He held in his hands a beautiful handwritten manuscript which he was reading with great concentration. Yet from the corner of his eye he saw me. He didn't know who I was but he was surprised to see a lone boy entering his room. He sensed my unease.

"What is it, child? Do you want something?" gurudev asked gently.

"I am very unhappy." I said, "My mother is crying. She has been crying for the past four years. She is full of sorrow."

"What happened to her?" gurudev inquired.

"My father died four years ago. That has left her unsettled. Is there a way by which one could stop the demon of death making people cry?"

"This is a very good question. This world is a continuous cycle of birth and death. There is no end to it." On this occasion gurudev did not seem to wish to elaborate. He did not seem to think that a little boy like me needed any further explanation. But I wanted more. I wanted him to tell me that yes, there is a way to stop death. I believed that if anyone knew the answer it was gurudev Tulsi.

"But there must be a way out of death."

"Yes there is a way. Do you want to know that way?"

"Yes, gurudev, I do."

"The way is to renounce the world. This is what we monks have done. We have embarked upon an arduous journey to end death and birth." This was a very bold answer. Renounce the world! Leave my mother behind? Leave my dear sister Suraj behind? Leave my teacher Gopalji behind? A string of questions reeled out in my head, and every time the answer was Yes, Yes. I should do everything to defeat the demon of death.

"I want to be a monk too. I will do anything. I will follow your path."

"Such decisions cannot be taken in a hurry. Go and think about it. Talk to your mother."

I LEFT THE ROOM in a sombre mood. I decided not to ask my mother at that moment; if my father's death had caused so much sorrow in her, what would be her response if I left her? This thought shook me deeply.

After a few days of being in Ladnun we returned to Shri Dungargarh. But my heart was left behind.

From this time on I became an even keener listener to Mother's stories and often asked for more.

"Mother, the other day you were telling me about learning from bees. Please tell me more about them."

"The bee teaches us," Mother said, "the way of pollination. We cannot find our fulfilment by ourselves; we depend on each other. Man depends on woman; I depend on you. I am grateful to you, my son, that you have come into the world through me. You needed my body to be born. I needed you so that I could be a mother. We humans depend on trees and rain and on the fruits of the earth. We need to work to strengthen the relationship between us and all life. That is the nature of pollination."

"Mother, who taught you about bees being our teachers?" I asked.

"Mahavir taught us to be like the honeybee. He went, begging for his food, from door to door and from household to household, always taking just a little. If someone offered him two pieces of bread, he would accept only one. No householder could ever say that a begging monk had taken all their food, that they had been left hungry, that they had been forced to cook again. Mahavir would go once a day to a dozen doors to get enough for a single meal.

"It was as though he had learnt the great virtue of restraint from the honeybee.

"Mahavir was like the bee, a great pollinator of wisdom. He went alone, always walking barefoot, carrying no possessions, not even a beg-ging bowl, and he brought stories and dreams, myths and meanings to peasants and princes, to poor and wealthy. Walking the earth has always been a most sacred act—a form of continuous pilgrimage for every *tirthankara.*

"Who is a tirthankara?" I asked.

"A tirthankara is one who makes a path through a river, who builds a ford, who helps you to cross the river and reach the other shore. The twenty-four Jain tirthankaras are the enlightened masters. They all walked up and down the land of India, covering thousands of miles.

"The tirthankaras, communing and meditating upon nature, roamed through the wilderness with a deep sense of the wonder and mystery of life. Countless mystical experiences in the natural world brought them enlight-enment."

"But how did the tirthankaras became enlightened?" I asked. To which she replied, "Because they lived in the wilderness, sat under the trees and communed with nature."

"Are there any tirthankaras alive today?" I was very excited

"No," Mother said sadly. "Because we have cut ourselves off from nature, and live in buildings in towns and cities. Even the monks no longer go much to the mountains and sit under the trees to learn from them. The tirthankaras spent long periods meditating in caves, in the mountains, and all of them went to the mountains to die.

"These mountains are sacred to the Jains, but nowadays Jains only go to the mountains where the tirthankaras died. This is a pity. The mountains are sacred not because the tirthankaras died there, but it is because the mountains are themselves sacred that the tirthankaras chose to die there. Of course, those mountains where the tirthankaras left their bodies are dear to the Jains, but we should not forget that all mountains are sacred."

"Which are the mountains where the tirthankaras passed away?" I asked.

"There are six," Mother said. "Mount Abu, Mount Shatrunjaya, Mount Girnar, Mount Rajgir, Mount Sammesdshikhar and Mount Kailash. Lord Mahavir died near Rajgir."

"When Mahavir walked to Rajgir, he walked barefoot, treading lightly on the earth. He kept his eyes on the ground to avoid stepping on any liv-ing creature. And if by mistake he stepped on any form of life, the harm would be less because he walked barefoot. Not injuring any life was his greatest concern and passion.

"Such was his reverence for life that he taught his disciples to refrain from eating any kind of meat or fish. His concern for life went even further.

He asked his followers to avoid eating roots because in order to eat a root, one has to dig up the whole plant. Grains, beans, peas, pulses and fruit are suitable foods, whereas onions, garlic, potatoes, carrots and similar root vegetables are not.

"Mahavir taught his followers that when they prepared fruit and vegetables containing multiple seeds, such as melon and pepper, they should remove all the seeds carefully for re-sowing and regeneration. Jains should always save seed. Where it was not easily possible to save the seed, such as with tomatoes and aubergines, then these vegetables should be avoided. Saving seed was the teaching of Adinath, the first tirthankara. Adinath taught that farmers should always sow more than they need so that there is enough for birds, mice and insects. When peas, pulses and grains are harvested, farmers should keep enough seed for sowing the following year and also leave seed on the ground for wildlife. In times of scarcity wild creatures should be fed." Now I knew why Mother would put grain on the top of an anthill. "We should be kind to all creatures," she said.

It was no accident that Mother revered Adinath as her favourite tirthankara, because he was the first to practise agriculture.

Avoidance of eating seeds and roots did not mean that food was a dull affair in our home. Each time Mother prepared a meal it was a minor feast. The aroma of spices, the colour of the foods, the manner of presentation, the ritual of eating and the care given to each member of the family made every day an occasion of celebration. Mother believed that "if you have bad food in your belly, you cannot have good thoughts in your head."

I never knew the taste of onions and garlic, potatoes and carrots in my childhood, and yet I remember the delights and pleasures of home cooking; the fewer the ingredients the greater the challenge to the imagination and to the art of the cook.

A YEAR AFTER WE WENT to Ladnun we were delighted that gurudev Tulsi himself, together with a group of his fellow monks, came to our town. This renewed encounter with him created a longing for liberation in my heart. I often thought of that day in Ladnun when for the first time I had heard the challenging words, "Renounce the World". After many conversations with gurudev, after many trials and tribulations, after many setbacks and discouragements, and after months of soul-searching, I was able to persuade my mother to let me join the order.[3]

So I became a monk.

Now it was possible for me to practise the path of freedom rather than talk about it. It is the practice which precedes the teaching. In the English language we talk about theory and practice, but in the Jain language it is practice then theory—*achar* then *vichar*. Theory must grow out of practice, out of a lived experience. There can be many theories about a practice, but it is the practice of compassionate living (*dharma*), which is the path of liberation. That is why the head of a Jain order is not one who is a scholar, a teacher or a writer, but 'the one who practises' (*acharya*). Our gurudev was called Acharya Tulsi.

"The practice of compassionate living (dharma)," said gurudev, "is not something other than everyday, ordinary, simple and mundane actions. This practice is in walking, in talking, in eating, in sleeping, in washing the bowl, in taking care of clothes, and in relating to all other beings. Compassion is not a matter of scholarship: you *live* it rather than you learn *about* it, think *about* it, or speak *about* it. It is like swimming: however many books you read about swimming, you will never be a swimmer until you get into the water, and the water gets into your eyes, your ears and your nostrils, and you swallow it. You think you are about to drown; but you don't drown, you move your arms and legs and you feel that you are all right, water is not there to drown you, it is there to hold you. There may be a swimming teacher to encourage you and give you confidence that if something untoward happens, he or she will come and rescue you, but you know that it is not the teacher but you who has to swim. The same is true with the practice of dharma. You have to jump into it.

"The essential practice of dharma is the practice of compassion to all bodies, such as earth body, fire body, water body and air body, because these natural bodies are not distinct from human bodies. Human bodies are made of these natural bodies. These natural bodies sacrifice themselves to nourish and sustain the human body. Therefore, it is the dharma of the human body to see the sanctity of the entire living order and respect the integrity of all beings. This is the first step towards the practice of dharma."

LORD MAHAVIR, the founder of the present-day Jain tradition, did not place much emphasis on studying or theorising. It was through the practice of compassion and non-violence that he communicated. When he taught, which he always did in a grove of trees or a forest, it is said that not only human beings would come to hear him, but also lions and deer, eagles and doves, peacocks and parrots, elephants and tigers, would all sit at his feet. Mahavir could communicate with animals because he was moved by love for animals as much as by love for people.

Mahavir was born a prince and lived in the luxury of his palatial home, but he found that despite having everything a person can desire he was deeply unhappy. The wealth and power was a cage of gold, but a cage nevertheless. People are trapped in the illusion that power and wealth can bring fulfilment. Recognising this illusion, he had the courage to abdicate and to seek liberation (*moksha*). He left his family, his servants and attendants, his horses and carriages, his security and comfort, never to see them again. He set off on an heroic journey of self-realisation. People thought that he was sacrificing privilege and power, but for him it was no sacrifice, it was a relief. People called him Maha Vir—Great Hero. To Mahavir it was easy enough to conquer others, rule over others and control others, but it was more difficult to conquer one's own ego, rule over one's own desires and control one's own passions.

* * *

Chapter 8

The Five Practices

THE DAY I TOOK the white robe of a monk gurudev Tulsi called me, together with some other young and newly robed monks, to receive religious instruction. He sat on a low wooden seat, and we settled down on a soft blanket on the floor.

"I will teach you", he said, "the basic practices of a monk, which can set your souls free. Mahavir followed these heroic practices, and we should do the same, in order to be free of the bondage and anguish caused by our petty desires.

"There are five principles you need to remember. The first is non-violence (*ahimsa*) which means doing no harm to yourself or to others. It is the avoidance of harmful thought, harmful speech and harmful action. It involves freeing oneself from all ill will and refusing to entertain any negative thought. In practice it means avoiding contact with the scenes of cruelty, malicious speech and activities which cause pain. You, the practitioners, should develop a discipline which enhances good will, positive thought, gentle speech and loving action."

There was a pause; then my fellow monk Tara, asked, "How can we learn to be like this?"

Gurudev answered, "Restraint is the key: think less, speak less, and do less. Be more, meditate more. Practise silence and serve others."

Another, longer, pause followed. I wondered if gurudev had forgotten what he was going to say next, so with impatience I asked, "What is the second principle?"

"Are you in a hurry? Have you understood the first principle? All right then, it is truth (*satya*), which means understanding the true nature of existence, including the true nature of oneself: accepting reality as it is and being truthful to it, attempting to see things as they are without judging them as good or bad. It means 'Don't lie' in its deepest sense, don't have illusions about yourself: how important you are, how unimportant you are, how good you are, how bad you are. Suspend all judgements. Face the truth without fear. Things are as they are; they are not good or bad, weak or strong. These are all interpretations."

Even though we were young novices, gurudev did not think we were incapable of understanding such profound thoughts. He was sowing seeds in our minds, which would flourish in the fullness of time. Gurudev continued, "A person of truth goes beyond mind, beyond words and realises existence as it is. Living in truth means that we avoid manipulating circumstances, people or nature to suit our own desires. We accept that other people have their own truth because there is no one single truth which any mind can grasp or tongue can express. Truth is the twin of 'no *one* conclusion' (*anekhant*). Most religions appear to believe that there is one truth, and the wise speak it in different ways. But the Jain perception is that reality is multi-centred. Each person, each tree, each flower, is a centre in an infinite universe. There can be neither one centre nor one truth. No monism."

"How can I know", asked monk Tara, "that I am being truthful, if there is no one truth?"

Gurudev replied, "Being truthful involves being humble and open to new discoveries and yet accepting that there is no final or ultimate discovery. Truth is what is. Mentally, verbally and physically we accept what is, as it is, speak of it as it is and live it as it is. There is no need to impose our view of what should be. Any individual or group claiming to know the *whole* truth is engaged in falsehood."

"But if we speak truth as we know it, can it not be hurtful to others?" I asked.

"There is a paradox here. You should speak the truth without fear, but you should learn to speak it sweetly. You should be honest, open and transparent. You must not hide behind platitudes, nor look the other way when faced with untruths. This is the essential skill you have to learn as a monk. Your truth should emerge from your deep well of compassion. Therefore, while speaking the truth you must avoid harsh words, you must speak the truth and yet be flexible. You must be prepared for the possibility that you might have got it wrong. You must be prepared to change your perception and your views when you find you were mistaken. Beyond this, you need to recognise that others have their own truth."

Gurudev had the habit of pausing during his teachings, to allow space and time for us to absorb the meaning of his words. So we waited until he was ready to speak again. After a while he said, "The third principle is not to steal *(asteya)*. This means refraining from acquiring things beyond your essential needs. It is difficult to know what your essential needs are, so you should assess your possessions, examine and question your life, day by day, to know what is your need. The distinction between need and greed can be blurred and therefore the examination of need should be carried out with honesty.

"The trading of goods has to be based on fair exchange, by which the labour, time and skill of the parties involved are measured by just and fair terms.

"If you take before giving it is stealing; so as monks, before you go out to beg for your food you should give your teaching, your guidance and your blessings. You help those who are in confusion, turmoil or depression. After helping others, you may receive from others."

After this brief explanation of the third principle, gurudev spoke about the fourth: "You should practise chastity and abstinence (*brahmacharya*). *Brahma* means pure being and *charya* means to dwell; hence chastity is to dwell in purity. This is the principle of love without lust. For lay people it means fidelity in marriage, and for monks it means total abstinence. Any thought, speech or act which demeans, debases or abuses the body is against the principle of chastity (brahmacharya). The body is the temple of pure being and therefore no activity should be undertaken which would defile this temple.

"Chastity extends the sanctity of the human body to the body of nature. Since Brahma, the pure being, is the essential principle of nature and permeates it, nature is the body of Brahma. To recognise the sacredness of existence is to live in fidelity with nature, which means being respectful to it, in the knowledge that it is not other than oneself."

Gurudev closed his eyes and breathed slowly for a few minutes. Then he spoke again: "The fifth principle is non-accumulation and non-possessiveness (*aparigraha*). You should not own anything; everything belongs to itself. Take what you need and leave the rest to itself. If no one hoards, owns, possesses or accumulates anything, then there will be no shortage of anything. Nature is abundant.

"This (aparigraha) is a way of sharing. Just as the members of a household living together as a family share everything, without a sense of private ownership, you too need to have no private ownership.

"Aparigraha is to live simply, without ostentation, without display of wealth. The dress, food and furnishing should be simple, elegant, but austere. Simple in means, rich in ends. If you spend too much time in accumulation and care of possessions, there will be no time left for care of the soul.

"Aparigraha also applies to ideas, knowledge, philosophy and religious thoughts. Acquisition of such nonmaterial possessions becomes spiritual materialism and they can be the most tightly binding of all possessions. Keep simple both your outer life and your inner thoughts."

After his usual pause, gurudev asked, "Do you have any questions?"

Although I was quite talkative with Mother, I felt shy with gurudev, particularly when he wanted me to ask questions. But monk Tara was not so shy. He bowed to gurudev and then asked, "Won't these ideals be difficult for people who live in the midst of the ordinary world?"

"These principles can be practised in two ways," said gurudev. "Monks and nuns follow these principles more strictly. For example, monks do not grow food, nor cook. We do not use any form of transportation other than our legs—not even a boat. If there is no bridge over a river, we do not go to the other shore. We do not touch money; we do not use candles or electricity, nor light a fire. We do everything by daylight and at night we chant and meditate in the dark. Monks make only minimal use of material resources."

"Some monks do not even wear clothes," I said.

"Yes, you are right; they are monks of the 'sky-clad' (*digambara*) order," observed gurudev. "They use their cupped hands as their begging bowl and have no possessions other than a peacock feather broom, with which to remove insects from their path or their body, and a wooden bowl for water. But we, the white-robed (*shwetambara*) are less extreme. We use two unstitched lengths of cloth, two blankets, three begging bowls and a few manuscripts of religious texts."

Gurudev continued, "But the lay people are less strict. Yet even for them, the acquisition of every pot, chair, table or any other goods, is a religious decision. Materialism cannot lie comfortably with Jainism. Jains limit the type and quantity of food they consume each day and they restrict the number of clothes they wear. Each day involves limiting consumption. For a Jain to shop or not to shop is a religious decision. And always the life of the monk or the nun sets the standard. A Jain is always weighing 'having' against 'being', and quality of life is always put before standard of living."

"Why live in such severe austerity?" asked monk Tara.

"This kind of austere lifestyle was preached by Mahavir, whose philosophy was about the appropriate place of the human being in the natural scheme of things. Keeping the population small through chastity (brahmacharya), and keeping consumption limited through non-acquisition (aparigraha), maintains equilibrium in the world. When there is greater equilibrium there is greater freedom from fear. Being free of violence, of falsehood, of theft, of indulgence and of possessiveness, sets you free."

Tara bowed twice, and said, "I am grateful to you, gurudev, for your answer. Would you kindly guide us further and tell us why we should seek freedom?"

Gurudev answered, "There is a vast world beyond the grasp of the five senses, and a journey into that world, the world beyond, the world of infinite mystery, can be experienced only when you are free from the bondage of the petty passions of this world. You seek freedom from this confined world of the senses, so that you can experience the universe of mystery.

"We will not be able to discover that universe if we are solely occupied and bound with the world of sensual gratification, which harbours dissatisfaction, discontentment, disappointment. The world of the senses, the world of ideas and opinions, the world of politics and commerce hold us back. Freedom from these enables us to go beyond.

"Respect matter, but be free from materialism. Obsession with matter, seeing nothing beyond matter, looking at matter as if it were there for human control, comfort and convenience, is materialism. Valuing humans on the basis of their material possessions—valuing people for what they 'have' rather than who they 'are', and valuing matter for what use it can be put to rather than for what it is—is also materialism. Being in the grip of such materialistic ideology can blind us from seeing the complete picture.

"When you are guided by the spirit you have no desire to fight over the acquisition of land, property and power. Jains do not fight wars; to be free they help evil to be transformed into good. They employ peaceful methods to resolve conflicts. They forgive those who follow the way of violence. They ask for forgiveness from those whom they may have harmed. Thus Jains free themselves from hate and anger."

I bowed humbly and asked, "But, gurudev, it is so easy to get sucked into anger and resentment. How can we be relieved from it?"

"Once a year," gurudev answered, "we have a 'Day of Forgiveness'. On that day all Jains fast for twenty-four hours, during which they reflect on the past year and remember any harmful acts they have committed against any beings: earth, air, fire, water, animals, humans. As they recall each act, they ask for forgiveness. When all the harmful acts have been remembered, they go to those people whom they have harmed or offended in thought, word or deed and declare that they have come in person to seek forgiveness: 'I have forgiven you, I bear no grudge against you, I harbour no animosity or feud in my heart, I am your friend and I have no enemies hereafter. I ask you to forgive me in the same spirit.' When these visits have been made, the person also writes letters to those he or she cannot visit in person. And when all this has been completed, then and only then is a Jain allowed to break his or her fast.

"This is like wiping the slate clean. By freeing yourself from the past you can live your life afresh. What a relief it is to breathe the air of freedom!"

We all bowed to gurudev, and that day's teaching came to a close.

* * *

Chapter 9

Self and the World

A YEAR AFTER I had joined the monkhood, when I was ten years old, Mother came for the *darshan* of gurudev Tulsi, so I asked him, "My mother wishes to see me and talk to me. May I have your permission to be with her?"

"She *was* your mother, but no longer. Remember you have renounced the world, including your mother!" gurudev reminded me.

"Yes, sir, I am sorry." Having received the permission I spent an hour or so talking with Mother-who-was. Now I called her by her name, Anchi, and she called me *muni-shri*, which meant Silent One, rather than 'my son'.

I noticed a melancholy in Anchi's face. Even though she was a wise woman, a keen observer of nature and skilled in human relationships, she was not so capable of coping with the absence of her son. It was a surprise to me that she was lost for words, so I initiated the conversation.

"Gurudev is so kind to me. He is giving a lot of time to teach me. Only this morning he spoke about the three kinds of relationships: The first is a relationship of harmony in personal love, which is called *raag*, like *raag* in music where sounds and notes are in accord. Secondly there is abstinence from relationships, in which one deliberately renounces personal love and attachment. This is called *viraag*. This may be a necessary stage but it is not the ideal, because one is trying to escape from the attachment to relationships. Then there is a third stage, the stage of tranquillity where one is neither attached to nor escaping from relationships. One is naturally joyful and at ease. This is called *veetraag*. In this state of liberated relationships one can engage with the world without getting caught up in it. You too, Anchi, spoke about this some time ago."

"Yes I did," Anchi remembered, "but I think I am still at the second stage, attempting to escape from attachment (viraag)." This answer revealed her state of mind. She appeared to have lost her usual vigour and self-confidence. I felt somewhat responsible for this. In looking for my own liberation had I unsettled Anchi?, I wondered. Certainly, I was not at ease with myself either. Therefore I was in the state of attachment (raag). But I had burned my bridges, there was no going back, so I suppressed my feelings and spoke serene words, copying my teacher.

"Gurudev spoke about being fully aware of your feelings, your speech and your actions. He said that often people live mindlessly, like sleepwalkers, not totally aware of what they are doing and the consequences of their thoughts and actions. They act out of past habits rather than from deep consciousness. It is a state of sleep in which things are happening as in a dream. In order to discover the third stage of relating to the world (veetraag), one needs to wake up, pay full attention to the minutest movement of mind, body and heart. Only an awakened being can arrive at the state beyond likes and dislikes; a state of unconditional love, love without discrimination or judgement."

Suddenly Anchi seemed more like her normal self. There was a spark of energy in her eyes. She said, "Gurudev is absolutely right. This awakening can happen only when we are able to live in the present moment. My problem is that from time to time I revert to the past, to the days when your father was alive and even to the days when you were with me. But I know that the past is past, the only reality is this moment. Past is only a memory, future is only in our imagination. The past and the future are products of our minds. Soul is always in the present, and the soul is the home of tranquillity. Only soul can experience the state beyond likes and dislikes, and that experience can happen only in the Now. Likes and dislikes are the result of a collection of past memories and of future plans. If we pay attention and if we are awake, then we can be in a state beyond delusions (veetraag). Gurudev is so right." I was delighted to hear such vigorous words flowing from Anchi's mouth. As she used to give examples from nature to talk about spirituality, she did so now:

"I think water is a good example. It does not say 'I will only quench the thirst of a good person, and I will deny my refreshing qualities to a bad person.' Water makes no judgement, it just is, and that to me is a perfect example of veetraag.

"Earth too practises the same equanimity. Farmers dig it, builders build upon it, and we all trample on it. Yet the earth forgives us all. The earth nourishes all kinds of trees. It does not make rules as to how the trees should grow or what kinds of trees and plants there should be. It does not control whether there is apple or orange, mango or melon, rice or wheat. The earth does not discriminate between brambles and roses. The earth serves all. This is the compassion (*dharma*) of the earth.

"Air also is beyond likes or dislikes. It carries all smells, good or bad. It gives life to all, whether a king or a slave, an elephant or a worm, air nourishes them equally.

"Space treats the world with similar evenness. Whether we try to build a Taj Mahal or a tiny hut, whether we plant a mango tree or a thorny bush, space discriminates against nothing and accommodates everything.

"And so it is with fire. It will burn whatever we put in it. Thus we can learn to practise like the natural elements and be our natural selves."

Anchi's insights complemented the teachings of gurudev. His explanations came from the old texts of Jain tradition and from the life of Mahavir, whereas Anchi's observations were part of her own experience. It came from listening to the voice of the land, as she worked on the land. She listened to the animals, birds, bees and trees. She was a true listener (*shravika*). In the Jain tradition the lay women are called *shravika* and the lay men *shravaka*, meaning listeners.

As a monk I was called 'the silent one' (*muni*). So the monks, teachers of religion, keep silence, and lay people, who are the disciples, listen. Communication happens without words. When lay people come for the experience of being in the presence of the monks (darshan), or of an image in a temple, no words are exchanged. Just being in the presence of a sacred image or a holy person is enough.

It is said that Mahavir did not speak, yet angels, humans, animals, and plants understood him in their own language. His presence was a catalyst for people to awaken themselves and find their own inner wisdom. Those who could understand him did not need him to speak, and those who were incapable of understanding would not understand any better, however much he might speak.

There is a story: a religious teacher was invited to speak at a gathering. He asked the crowd if they knew what he was going to speak about. They shook their heads in ignorance. The teacher said, "If you have no idea at all, then what is the use of my talking to you—you will not understand," and he went home. The second day he was invited again, and he repeated the question. This time the answer came, "Yes".

"Well, if you already know, what is the use of my telling you?" and again he went home. The third day the audience was better prepared. They replied to his question, "Some of us do and some of us don't."

"In that case," said the teacher, "let those who do tell those who don't."

Just being present in the company of Mahavir and paying full attention to that moment enabled people's innate knowledge to be uncovered and to unfold. Knowledge is not outside oneself, it is already there. It is covered with a golden disk of illusions. By being aware, awake, and present in the moment one is able to release the free spirit within. That is why Mahavir was called Mahamuni, the Great Silent One. It is more often the case that preachers preach and the audience don't listen, and much energy is wasted. So the deep listening is to listen to that which cannot be spoken in words. When we are in the state beyond likes and dislikes (veetraag), we are able to listen deeply.

YEAR AFTER YEAR for eight years Anchi would come and visit, and we continued these conversations until I was eighteen years old, when I read the autobiography of Mahatma Gandhi. I had been a monk for nine years. By that time the anguish about death had receded and Gandhi's story stirred me at the core of my being. He raised a thousand and one questions in my head. Anchi had come to visit me and I wanted to tell her something of what I had just learned about Gandhi's way of thinking.

"Essentially, Gandhi says that it is no good some people renouncing the world and joining a monastic order, others going off to the Himalayas to live in a cave, both engaging in a search for God, thinking that the world is a trap, a dirty place, a place of sin, and that only by escaping from it can one find salvation, while at the same time there are masses of ordinary people living in the world and thinking that spirituality is only for the saints." This puzzled Mother. She could hear some notes of discontent in my voice.

"Of course we all try to practise dharma, spiritual and ethical living, but under the social and economic pressures of life it is not possible for us to practise dharma fully. Only the monks can devote themselves entirely to the way of compassion (dharma)," Mother countered.

"But Gandhi says that if monks and nuns alone can obtain salvation (*moksha*) then spirituality becomes the prerogative of the few, a privileged elite, while the majority of people are disempowered. He thinks that we need to find a way of salvation which is accessible to all people, everywhere. We need to liberate spirituality from the monasteries, caves, and religious institutions and bring it to all people. Spirituality needs to be part of everyday life. Non-violence and truth is not something special to be practised by special people. We need to bring non-violence and truth into politics, business, agriculture, and into our homes.

"For Gandhi that spirituality is no spirituality which does not bring an end to injustice, exploitation and social divisions. That love is no love which does not embrace the untouchables, the slum dwellers, and the artisans. Love of God and love of people cannot be put into separate compartments."

This was a kind of social spirituality. As a monk I was practising an individual spirituality for the purpose of my personal purity. My non-violence was a personal non-violence. Gandhi was extending that personal non-violence into a collective or social non-violence. Gandhi's non-violence was positive and active; act against the violent systems and tendencies which create division between self and other, between rich and poor, between upper and lower castes.

Gandhi himself had been greatly inspired by Jain teachings. Therefore, his non-violence and Jain non-violence were totally complementary. Gandhi believed that if all life is one, then I cannot and should not undermine the dignity of the other. All social, political and economic relationships need to be built on this fundamental principle of reverence for all life. If our society is built on the foundation of non-violence and spirituality, then every human individual will tend to act in a compassionate manner. There will be no need for rules of morality or religious directives. According to Gandhi, this division between religious orders and worldly life is the cause of many of our sufferings.

Being compassionate to others is also being compassionate to ourselves. When we are violent to others we are violent to ourselves. When we denigrate or demean others, we denigrate and demean ourselves. Anger disturbs the angry person more than it upsets the recipient of that anger.

Non-violence is the soil in which the tree of love grows. When we practise non-violence, truth finds us; we need not go searching after it. Having spent much of his life and his energy in experimenting with truth, Gandhi realised that it is in the relationship of non-violence with all beings that truth is found. Non-violence is the defining measure of our relationship with other humans and the natural world. If it is based on non-violence, then that relationship is right relationship. Whether one is a monk or living an ordinary life should not matter.

DETECTING A HINT of despondency in my voice, Anchi advised me to talk to gurudev and seek clarification. She believed in the importance of monks setting a greater and purer example for lay people, in contrast to Gandhi's idea that there should be no division between lay people and monks.

So I spoke to gurudev, and despite receiving his advice I remained convinced that renouncing the world could not save the soul, I believed that seeking personal salvation was a selfish way of approaching spiritual realisation. Gandhi's arguments had had a very powerful effect on me.

When the Buddha, after his enlightenment, reached the gates of Nirvana, it is said that he was welcomed by the angels at the door. But before entering he had a moment of reflection. He looked around and saw the world in suffering. He said to the angels, "How can I enter these gates of Nirvana while the earthly beings are in turmoil?" Overwhelmed with compassion, the Buddha declined to take his place in Nirvana and decided to remain on Earth until all sentient beings were free of pain, anguish and suffering.

I was deeply moved by this noble legend. Nirvana is not somewhere outside the world; it is here in offering ourselves to the others in such a way that there is no self and there is no other. This realisation itself is nirvana. In this teaching of the Buddha I felt as if he was the twenty-fifth *tirthankara*, the great spiritual teacher in line with Mahavir.

So I decided to leave the monastic order and seek what I called post-religious spirituality. Acting in this way I did not feel that I was abandoning the teachings of Mahavir, nor the way of the Jains. In leaving the monkhood I was leaving only the formal and institutionalised life of a monk. For me, Gandhi was reinvigorating and renewing the essential message of Mahavir. To me he was almost like the twenty-sixth tirthankara. I wanted to practise dharma in the world, not pretend to be outside it: no one can be outside the world, for renouncing the world is a contradiction in terms.

I had left home because I was afraid of death. After nine years of walking, studying, meditating, observing and paying attention to the intricate workings of life, I began to understand that there is no beginning of life and there is no end to life; all is change of form. Where there were oceans, now there are deserts, mountains have become plains, and dark bitter soil becomes sweet and fragrant fruit. It is all a continuous transformation—no birth, no death. Earth, air, fire, water, space, time and consciousness constantly forming, reforming, deforming, informing and transforming. So death ceased to concern me. But being bound by the structure of a religious order created yet another longing for liberation.

* * *

PART TWO

Quest
for Wholeness

From you I receive, to you I give.
Together we share, by this we live.

—Anon

The only wisdom we can hope to attain is humility;
humility is endless.

—T. S. Eliot

Chapter 10

Return to the World

Solvitur ambulando (it is solved by walking)
—St. Augustine

ONE NIGHT AFTER midnight, when the town was asleep, I escaped from the order. I wanted to join the Gandhians. But before that I wanted to see Mother, who had been 'Anchi' for so long. I returned home with trepidation. For Mother the news of my departure from the monastic order was a devastating blow. During the years I had been away, Mother had taken on many new responsibilities. She had become deeply engaged in the religious community of the Jains. She had found a new lease of life in organising events, planning the visits of monks to our town and co-ordinating groups going for *darshan* of gurudev. She had become a stalwart of the community.

When I took the vow of monkhood it was for life. Breaking that vow was not something the Jain community was able to accept. And Mother could not accept what her fellow Jains would not accept. Despite her love for me and her free spirit, her commitments to the community would not allow her to associate with me, or let me return home.

"You have brought shame upon me! You have broken your lifelong vows!", Mother cried.

"Yes I have, but those vows were no longer commitments of my heart. They turned into an outer façade. Something within me has totally changed."

"Maybe someone has misguided you. Did you speak to gurudev? He would have cleared your doubts."

"I have derobed myself because the monk's robe was separating me from the world," I said.

"But one needs a form. One needs to anchor oneself somewhere. That form need not be a burden. You can be in the form and yet free of it. Do you remember our discussions about being beyond likes and dislikes (the state of *veetraag*)? In that state wherever you are, whatever the outer conditions, they do not imprison you. In fact you can be free even in prison!

Why do you bring this shame on me and our family by breaking your vows and your commitments? Freedom is not related to external conditions, it is part of your inner being. Moreover, how painful it will be for gurudev to lose a disciple like you. He has spent nine precious years teaching you."

"But gurudev was not teaching me for any selfish gain. Surely he himself must be in the state of veetraag, of detachment. He cannot be upset because someone is leaving him, or pleased because someone is joining him. Surely he is beyond all that," I tried to reason.

"He may be beyond all attachments, but it is not up to you to judge him, and use his detachment to defend your unworthy actions! Have you reciprocated his gifts to you? Have you fulfilled your obligations, your duties, your responsibilities?" Mother was obviously angry.

"I am very sorry if I have upset you, Mother. I know the members of our community will talk badly of me and that will hurt you. But I must listen to my own inner voice, follow my own path. It will not be right for me to do or not to do something just because people will be criticising me. I am harming no one. I am longing for liberation. I want to know, who am I, and what is my true path."

This was a very delicate moment. Mother was not upset about my actions *per se*; rather she was worried about the impact my actions would have on the Jain community. Moreover, she could not remain an active Jain and harbour a fallen monk in her house.

"If you wish to pursue your own path, then so be it. Take your own responsibility and go where you will. Now I am used to living without you and, in any case, if you were restless at home at the age of nine and restless as a monk at eighteen, what is going to stop you from being restless now, here with me?"

These words were clearly the words of parting.

IT WAS 1957. I was twenty-one. I went to Kerala in south India to meet Vinoba Bhave, whom I had met once before, while I was still a monk. If there was anyone who was embodying the vision of Mahatma Gandhi, who had integrated the concerns of the soul and those of the world and who also could be my friend and mentor, then it was Vinoba.

Even though I had travelled 3,000 miles from Rajasthan in the north to Kerala in the south, spiritually my journey from Tulsi to Vinoba was not very long. Tulsi and Vinoba were both seeking liberation. Tulsi's path was through soul to society, Vinoba's path was through society to soul.

I was intrigued by his name. 'Vinu' means humble and 'ba' means mother. 'Humble mother' in a man's body. Vinoba seemed to combine the qualities of my mother and my guru. And he was walking, walking everywhere. Mahavir had found his enlightenment while walking, Mother learned her wisdom from nature while walking, Tulsi taught me tranquillity while walking, and now Vinoba was walking the length and breadth of India, covering thousands of miles, to carry forward the unfinished work of Mahatma Gandhi. I found myself in the right place, with the right man, at the right time. I was very happy. It was a time of excitement and anticipation.

I met Vinoba in the town of Kaladi. He had done his day's walk. He was sitting on a cushion on the floor, reading a manuscript. There was a low table in front of him. On one side of it were a few books, the *Bhagavad Gita* being one of them. On the other side lay a notepad, a pen and a small clock. On the table was placed a brass mug, from which he sipped water from time to time. He was wearing a white loincloth and a piece of unstitched cloth around his torso. Occasionally he stroked his pointed white beard, which contrasted with his black hair. He had small, charming, bright eyes. His tall, frail body contained a robust mind and gentle personality. He was wearing a green cap and thick framed glasses.

I entered the room and sat down near Vinoba. One of his assistants invited me to introduce myself. I said, "For nine years I lived as a mendicant monk, barefoot, a begging bowl in my hand, searching for spirituality and seeking personal salvation. Yet I was restless. Gandhi's idea of integrating individual spirituality with social spirituality has moved me. Now I have come to be with you and be in the world, yet I wish to follow the way of the spirit."

In a consoling voice Vinoba said, "Rendering service to the world is not distinct from following a spiritual path. There is no difference between the two. The service to creation and the quest for spiritual realisation do not demand two different courses of action. When we are able to live and act without desiring 'the fruit' of our actions we are immediately on a spiritual path. Even though there is no *desire* for fruit in performing our daily actions, nevertheless they do yield noble fruit. But by simply relinquishing the *desire* for results, for achievement, for success, for gain, one is able to transcend the division between social action and spiritual action."

AFTER THIS BRIEF but reassuring encounter I went for a walk in the streets of the town. Reflecting on what Vinoba had said, I felt that fundamentally what my mother and Gopalji were teaching, and what I had learned from gurudev Tulsi, were coming together in Vinoba. There were no fundamental contradictions, although there were differences of emphasis.

Walking under the tall coconut trees was calming and relaxing. Never before had I seen coconut trees. A slim round trunk without any branches reached nearly a hundred feet up into the sky. It was a staggering sight. As the tree climbed upwards its roots went deeper into the soil. The coconut tree seemed to be living simultaneously in heaven and in earth, providing earthly fruit with a heavenly taste!

A woman with her son, a young man, managed a coconut stall. The fruit was elegantly stacked in small pyramids. It was impossible to resist the temptation to drink the fresh coconut juice. I could not speak the local language, Malayalam, but my sign language was enough to communicate. The young man cut off the top of the fruit and for the first time I drank the fresh juice and ate the soft coconut pulp. It was not too sweet, not too bland, totally refreshing. A great gift of nature.

Kerala was lush, luxuriant, green and abundant, the very opposite of the dry desert of Rajasthan. Stall after stall of pineapples and bananas lined the street. In the north of India, I had seen only two or three kinds of banana, but here there were dozens of varieties on display: cooking bananas, red-skin bananas, long bananas, short bananas—bananas galore. And then black pepper, cardamom, ginger, cinnamon, tea and coffee. There cannot be anything, I thought, which does not grow in Kerala. I felt I was in Paradise. My soul and body were nourished. I wished my mother had been there to experience this abundant beauty of the earth. She would have derived many meanings and metaphors from the splendour of nature in Kerala.

Vinoba had invited me to join his walk the next morning so that we could continue our conversation. I felt honoured and privileged. There were hundreds of highly regarded luminaries who were queuing to get a glimpse of Vinoba, and here I was, a young, inexperienced enthusiast getting his attention. Vinoba was obviously intrigued that I, a Jain monk, should seek his company.

He said, "You should read my *Talks on the Gita*.[4] Many of your perplexities will find answers there. It tells you how to join the outward with the inward."

"I will. But would you be so kind as to tell me how to know when one's actions are without desires?"

"If your actions are joyful and beautiful then they are pure. Beauty is the touchstone. If the action is performed with a pure heart, then beauty appears there. Beauty is the outcome of pure action. Good sculptors are fully present in the carving, totally absorbed in action, unaffected by speculations about how much they will sell the sculpture for, how much fame and recognition they will get when people see their work. All such future plans are suspended. Action is performed without desires. Then somehow, from somewhere, beauty emerges in the sculpture. Without that purity of heart how can the goddess of beauty manifest herself and bless the artist? The beauty of the image is nothing but the beauty of the sculptor's soul. If the sculptor's soul is beautiful then the image will also be beautiful," said Vinoba.

"But," I asked, "is it possible for ordinary people like me to attain such purity, such desirelessness?"

"Yes!" said Vinoba. "Anybody and everybody is capable of such action. When hands, heart and mind are integrated and soul is free of desires then every work becomes a work of art. Art is work well done, and work can only be done well when the person is free of attachment, ego and desires. We are all capable of such action."

There was a pause. Vinoba put his hand on my shoulder. After a short silence, changing the subject I said, "Going back to our conversation of yesterday, Vinoba, could you say something about the relationship between the individual and society?"

"It is impossible", Vinoba replied, "to separate these two. We cannot distinguish between the good of the individual and the good of society. If we look at the big picture, then it becomes clear that ultimately what is good for the individual is also good for society, and vice versa. There can be no conflict of interest here. It is like the air in the room and the unbound atmosphere without. There is neither difference nor conflict between these two. If we imagine that there is a conflict, and if we shut the doors and windows, we will only be suffocated to death. Therefore, the doors of the room must be left open to allow the boundless air to flow in. The moment we cut off individuals from the society and think that either spiritually or materially an individual can blossom without community, or the community can flourish without the contribution of individuals, we are misguided."

"But we are often told to stand on our own feet and fend for ourselves. What do you think of that?" I asked.

"Individuals fending only for themselves is hell," said Vinoba, "while individuals working together as a community, supporting each other, is heaven. There is a tale illustrating this point:

"Once, a man wanted to find out what hell and heaven were like. First he went to see hell. The place looked reasonably fine. People lived in their separate living quarters. When the dinner bell rang, all the individuals emerged from their rooms. They were tall people with long legs and long arms. They sat down on either side of a long table. They looked anxious and hungry. The food was fine too; rice, bread and vegetables were served. When they started to eat, they took some food in their spoons and tried to put it in their mouths, but because of their stiff long arms they could not reach their mouths, and the food kept going over their shoulder behind their back and falling on the floor. What was on the table now lay on the floor. The visitor was amused.

"Then the visitor went to heaven. The place did not seem that dissimilar. The residents all lived in a cluster of rooms around a courtyard. The visitor could hear conversations interspersed with laughter. Moments later the dinner bell rang. Tall people with long arms and legs came out of their rooms looking happy and sat down either side of the long table. Food was served; rice, bread and vegetables, exactly the same as in hell. But when they started to eat, instead of attempting to put food in their own mouths, each fed the person opposite. By feeding each other they made no waste, and their hunger was satisfied. The visitor was again amused."

IN 1957 KERALA WAS the first Indian state to elect a communist government. Therefore, the debate about the interests of the individual versus the interests of society was then at the top of the political agenda. On the one hand some people were of the opinion that if all individuals acted honestly, religiously, socially and morally, then society would take care of itself. On the other hand some people were arguing that it is the social structure which corrupts the individual; therefore, if we reform society, individuals will automatically behave well. They argued that in a capitalist system, individuals act out of self-interest, or they act in the interest of their class, rather than of society as a whole. In such a situation there is a conflict between the interest of the individual or class and those of the larger community.

Vinoba sought to transcend this dichotomy. "If the individual is to act without desire for personal gain, then his or her actions are bound to lead to the well-being of society, and at the same time such actions are personally satisfying and fulfilling," he said. "Transformation of the individual and transformation of society are therefore complementary. Communists need not put down those working for personal transformation, nor the latter put down the work of the communists. And if both work together non-violently and through democratic means, then they embrace a holistic perspective."

Vinoba continued: "Mahatma Gandhi coined the word *sarvodaya*. *Sarva* means all and *udaya* means well-being—not just well-being of an individual or the well-being of a community but of both and more. In a society based on the good of all (sarvodaya) there would be a constant conversation between the individual and the community. Community is, therefore the individual is. The individual is, therefore community is. Neither can exist without the other. Sarvodaya celebrates the individual without celebrating individualism. Sarvodaya also celebrates community without celebrating communism. Individualism sacrifices the community, while communism sacrifices the individual. Sarvodaya perceives the relationship between the two. Sarvodaya also means the well-being of animals, plants, insects and all other forms of life.

"Sarvodaya means the upliftment of all. It is a system which is designed to work for all. It is a radically different world-view from the paradigms of both Left and Right, or socialist and capitalist. Sarvodaya neither accepts the Marxist class analysis which claims that there is an inherent conflict of interest between the classes, nor does it accept the capitalist notion that people are primarily driven by economic self-interest.

"Sarvodaya pursues decentralised and small-scale community politics, one which safeguards the interest of the collective as well as the individual. Moreover, sarvodaya embraces the well-being of the Earth. Capitalism favours the few—only those who have capital. Socialism cares for the many—it believes in the greatest good of the greatest number, but some are still left out. Capitalism and socialism are both anthropocentric, whereas sarvodaya cares for all, and it cares for the weak and poor first, because they need help the most. Neither any humans nor any part of the natural world fall outside the ambit of sarvodaya. Capitalism is self-centred, socialism is society-centred, and sarvodaya is life-centred," he concluded.

*   *   *

Chapter 11

Soil, Soul, Society

I STARTED READING *Talks on the Gita,* as Vinoba suggested. The book is a collection of lectures delivered in Dhulia Jail when Vinoba was imprisoned by the British. Many political prisoners were there who had committed non-violent acts of civil disobedience alongside Vinoba during the struggle for India's independence. The inmates knew that Vinoba was a great scholar of the *Bhagavad Gita* and urged him to speak about it, to help them understand how their struggle was as much a spiritual process as it was a political process. The Indian guards of the jail were happy to permit and even join in these talks. Once a week Vinoba spoke about the meaning of the *Gita* and the philosophy which flows from it. One of his fellow prisoners wrote these talks down, and it is from these writings that the book emerged.

According to the *Gita,* nature, society and self form a triangle, an interconnected whole. Every day we need to take care of these three aspects of our lives.

The *Gita* gives us a guideline. It shows the appropriate relationship to nature, to human communities, and to ourselves. There are three key concepts: nourishing soil through *yagna,* nourishing society through *dana,* and nourishing the self through *tapas.*

Through yagna we make up the harm that we have caused to creation, and replenish it. To 'make good the loss' is yagna. For example, we annually plough the earth. In so doing there may be soil erosion, and a depletion of the natural nutrients. So when we give manure to the soil and when we allow the land to remain fallow for a year so that it may regain its fertility, then we are nourishing nature (yagna). To build a house we cut down trees. This is a loss to nature. So we plant not one tree—that would be mere replacement—but we plant five or more trees. That is replenishment, that is yagna.

The second concept is nourishing society through gifts (dana). We need to remember that from birth we are nourished by society. Our family and our community take care of us. Our teachers give us their knowledge. Art, culture and science are a collective gift from past and present generations. We in return offer our talents, our labour, our knowledge as a gift to society. That is dana.

Then there is the nourishing of the self. We replenish our body and soul through fasting, meditation, study, silence, rest and being in nature. Such attention to the self is tapas.

In truth, these three are not distinct. The self is not outside society, and society is not outside the natural world. These three together make up the beautiful order of the Earth. But for the sake of convenience Vinoba articulated these three categories from the *Gita*.

THIS TRINITY OF nourishing nature, society and self gave me much food for thought. Ever since that time they have remained with me and have become the ground of my thinking and action. I have chosen my own words for this trinity: 'Soil, Soul and Society'. Human aspirations have often been expressed in trinities. 'Father, Son and Holy Spirit' inspires the Christian vision. 'Life, Liberty and the Pursuit of Happiness' focussed American aspirations. 'Liberté, Egalité, Fraternité' drove the French Revolution. 'Mind, Body and Spirit' is at the heart of the 'New Age' movement. In what I refer to as the Age of Ecology, 'Soil, Soul and Society' can inspire a truly holistic thinking. They can bring nature, humanity and spirituality together.

'Father, Son and Holy Spirit' is a spiritual trinity, but it takes no note of the social and ecological dimensions.

In reaction to the dominance of the Christian trinity and against the established order of the time, 'Liberté, Egalité, Fraternité' was promoted as a social trinity. But the natural world and the spiritual dimensions are left out. In the wake of the Renaissance and the Enlightenment, humanism became the dominant philosophy: human freedom, human progress, human well-being and human rights were given prominence over reverence for nature and care of the soul. This was understandable in the seventeenth and eighteenth centuries, because dogmatic religious institutions ignored social justice, equality and democracy. Therefore, in the drive to liberate Europe from religious subjugation, humanism became the paramount concern of the time. So, together with religion, spirituality too was discarded.

The new age trinity of 'Mind, Body, Spirit' is a personal trinity. This too ignores the issues of social justice and ecological sustainability. The attempt for personal growth and personal fulfilment has resemblances to the 'monk's path', if somewhat more comfortable and self-indulgent. It is like looking in the mirror and wondering, "Why am I not looking well?" and forgetting that the fragmentation of society and the degradation of the natural world has an impact and an influence on our personal well-being.

Therefore, 'Soil, Soul, Society' is an inclusive and holistic trinity.

Soil must come first because we arise from the soil and we return to the soil. Our food, our everyday nourishment, grows out of the soil. All the materials we use to build houses come from the soil. If there was no soil we would have neither cotton nor wool for our clothes. Every fuel we use—oil, coal, gas and wood—comes from the soil. Our art and culture have been inspired by the natural world which is maintained by the soil. Soil represents the Earth, holds life and accommodates air, fire and water. Our sustenance depends on the soil. The soil is more than an object of utility, it is the symbol of life.

The Indian philosophers of ancient times composed philosophical treatises called the Upanishads. There they proclaimed[5] that all and everything, whatever there is, is the home of the divine. All things, in their natural state, are pure, all things holy. Nature has its own sovereign spirit. Animals, birds, rivers, mountains, gods and goddesses live together in an interdependent relationship. Their sanctity does not come from 'God' reigning somewhere above, but from the divine or sacred element which is inherent within.[6] Divinity is immanent in nature, not transcendent, not beyond nature. We human beings receive the bounty of nature as a divine gift. We are an integral part of nature. We are required to live upon the Earth with a sense of humility and gratitude. Caring and conserving the Earth is our responsibility not only because the Earth is useful to us, but because the Earth is sacred and good in itself. This I call Reverential Ecology.

The humanism which emerged out of the Renaissance, the Enlightenment, the industrial revolution, scientific progress and technological advancements has tended to create an arrogant conviction that the natural world exists for the benefit of humanity; that human beings are somehow superior to other forms of life; that they are in charge of the Earth, and can control, own, and use the Earth as they choose. This arrogant and anthropocentric world-view is at the root of the present ecological, social and spiritual crisis.

According to the *Gita*, the resolution of this crisis would be to take from the Earth only to meet our essential needs, and to replenish the losses we have caused.

I HAD JUST FINISHED reading *Talks on the Gita* and was discussing its content with Vinoba. He told me a story about Gandhi's practice of the *Gita*'s principles in minimising his own needs.

Mahatma Gandhi was once staying in the city of Allahabad with Mr Nehru, who later became the first Indian prime minister. There was no

running water in the house in those days. So Nehru brought a jug of water
for Gandhi's morning wash. Nehru was pouring water from the jug as
they talked about the political situation in India. As they were deeply
engaged in serious discussion, the jug of water finished before Gandhi
completed his wash. Nehru said, "Wait for a minute, let me fetch another
jug of water."

Gandhi was astonished. He said, "What! You mean I have used that
whole jug full of water without having finished washing my face? How
wasteful of me! I never use more than one jug of water for my morning
wash." Gandhi stopped talking. Nehru could not understand what the fuss
was about and why Gandhi was so serious. Moments later Nehru was even
more surprised; he saw tears in Gandhi's eyes.

"Why are you crying?" asked Nehru.

"I am too careless and wasteful. I am ashamed!"

"Here in the city of Allahabad there are two great rivers flowing—
Ganges and Yamuna. There is no shortage of water here. This is not your
state—Gujarat, the dry and desert land."

"You are right, here in your city you have plenty of water. You are
blessed to have two great rivers running through your city, but my share is
only one jug of water a day for my wash, and no more."

For Vinoba, this was an exemplary attitude towards nature. Gandhi
did not want to waste even a drop of water. Waste is one of the greatest
failings of the modern world. Waste is violence, a sin against nature.

In modern cities like New York or New Delhi there are mountains of
waste. Mass production causes mass waste: whether anyone needs those
products or not, factories must go on producing just to keep the production system going and to maintain the workers in employment. We take the
natural materials from the earth, make them into synthetic products and
throw them away often in a condition where they cannot be re-absorbed
by nature.

When work is performed with the soil in mind, there should be no
waste. In nature there is no waste. Scarcity is caused by depletion of the
soil, and depletion is caused by waste. If we are able to reuse, recycle and
replenish resources and use them with care and restraint, then there can
never be scarcity. Abundance is the law of nature. "There is enough in the
world for everybody's need, but not enough for anybody's greed," said
Gandhi. Greed and waste leads to scarcity. Care and restraint leads to
abundance.

Vinoba also spoke of the Buddhist practice of nourishing nature by
planting trees. He told me about the great Buddhist emperor of India,
Ashoka, who proclaimed that all citizens should plant a minimum of five

trees in their lifetime and look after them. He asked the citizens to include one medicinal tree, one fruiting tree, one tree for firewood, one hardwood tree for house-building, and one for flowers. He called it the grove of five trees (*panchavati*).

While walking in Kerala I noticed that some Christian families there decorated a tree at Christmas time as a symbol of reverence for trees. Unlike their European counterparts they did not remove their trees from the land, but decorated them outside where they stood. Christmas in Kerala is celebrated by the planting of trees.

AFTER NOURISHING NATURE comes the nourishing of society, which means a social order based on giving and receiving (dana). It means reciprocity and mutuality. We use intellectual, cultural and religious wealth to enrich our lives. This wealth has accumulated from generation to generation. We have learned much from the native Americans, the Australian Aboriginals, the indigenous people of India (*adivasis*) and the Bushmen of Africa.

We have been guided by Jesus Christ, The Buddha, Mohammed, and Mahavir. We have been inspired by Valmiki, Shakespeare, Tolstoy, Jane Austen and many other writers. We have benefited from the lives of Mahatma Gandhi, Mother Teresa and Martin Luther King. They were not motivated by fame, fortune or power. Buddha claimed no copyright on his teachings, and Shakespeare received no royalty cheques. We have been enchanted by music, paintings, architecture and crafts of many cultures, from time immemorial. We have received a treasure house of traditions as a free gift.

In return we offer our work, our creativity, our arts and crafts, our agriculture and architecture as gifts to society—to present and future generations. When we are motivated by this spirit then work is not a burden. It is not a duty. It is not a responsibility. We are not even the doers of our work. Work flows through us and not from us. We do not own our intellect, our creativity, or our skills. We have received them as a gift and grace. We pass them on as a gift and grace; it is like a river which keeps flowing. All the tributaries make the river great. We are the tributaries adding to the great river of time and culture; the river of humanity. If tributaries stop flowing into the river, if they become individualistic and egotistical, if they put terms and conditions before they join the rivers, they will dry and the rivers will dry too. To keep the rivers flowing all tributaries have to join in with joy and without conditions. In the same way, all individual arts, crafts and other creative activities make up the river of humanity. We need not hold back, we need not block the flow. This is unconditional union. This is the great principle of dana. This is how society and civilisations are replenished.

The poetry of Goethe and Milton, the myths of Mahabharata and King Arthur, the paintings of Van Gogh and Botticelli, the music of Mozart, the pyramids of Egypt, the Taj Mahal of India and thousands of other blossomings of creativity in the past have enriched us. We are filled with gratitude. Every moment is a moment of thanksgiving. This is our true 'capital' that we have inherited. But we cannot live off the capital for ever. If we do not replenish it, it will come to an end. It is good to cherish the fruits of our heritage, but it is a living imperative that we continue to add our creativity to this vital culture.

When we write a poem we make a gift. When we paint a picture or build a beautiful house we make a gift. When we grow flowers and cook food we make a gift. When all these activities are performed as sacred acts they nourish society. When we are unselfconscious, unacquisitive, and act without desire for recognition or reward, when our work emerges from a pure heart like that of a child, our actions become a gift, dana. But if our actions are performed with impure motives or for egotistical reasons, then however great the work may be, it is not a part of the nourishment of society, it is not dana.

Work done out of a pure state of mind is never a source of stress. Rather, work becomes a sustaining act (*dharma*), it is a source of joy and pleasure.

WHILE WE REPLENISH Soil and Society, we also need to replenish our Soul. Without caring for the soul we cannot care for the soil or society. There is a lot of wear and tear on our soul. Souls get wounded, sometimes by anger, other times by greed. Anxiety and fear damage the soul. Jealousy and resentment make our souls sick. Through rejection our inner world gets fragmented. The temptation of power corrupts our minds. Therefore, we need to heal our souls, to become whole and fulfilled. Tapas is the way of self-healing and self-purification.

When our bodies get sweaty and smelly we purify them by washing. When our clothes get dirty we wash them. When our rooms get dirty we sweep them clean. These practices help to purify our external environment, but what about the internal environment? We need some practices for inner purification. Our minds get polluted with harmful information. Newspapers and television agitate our minds. Our consciousness gets contaminated by ego and pride. Our souls get polluted by desires and anguish. so we need self-nourishment (tapas).

Solitude is one way of tapas. When we come in contact with the problems of the world—whether they are political, economic or domestic, we can be deeply affected by them. Constant contact with people, opinions and institutions puts a strain on our souls. Therefore, we go on a spiritual retreat or on a pilgrimage, where we are able to recover our serenity and return to our centre. Such solitude is particularly necessary in modern times when our diaries are full, our lives are busy, and we are constantly preoccupied with trivia. Meditation, silence of speech and mind, stillness of thought and body, being calm and restful, taking a break from the world of contradictions and complications, are ways of tapas.

Fasting is tapas. My mother, in her last years, made fasting a way of life. She would not eat on two days consecutively: she would eat one day and fast the next, which meant that for fifteen days of the month, in other words six months of the year, she fasted. Furthermore, once a year at par-ticular religious occasions she would fast for eight days.

Another form of fast among the Jains is to eat for one day and fast the next, eat for one day and fast for two days, eat for one day and fast for three, increasing the days of fasting up to fifteen. Then reverse the process, fasting for fourteen days, eating for one day, fasting for thirteen days, eat-ing for one day, and so on back to one. This is called the heat of austerity, a fire of wisdom to burn the mental clutter.

Another form of tapas is to eat slightly less than normal. If one has two slices of toast for breakfast, have only one, for example. If one eats three times a day, one decides to eat only twice, or once. Or one decides not to take second helpings. People limit the hours in which they will eat; the Jains do not eat after sunset, and Buddhist monks do not eat after midday.

Abstaining from excessive consumption is tapas. Reduction in the number of clothes, ornaments, shoes and other possessions is tapas. It also includes putting a limit on travels. Austerity is good for posterity. If we do not consume so many resources, then we do not deprive future generations. A simple and minimalist lifestyle is good for our health.

But self-replenishment (tapas) is not to be confused with suppression or repression or control. It is a positive concept with a positive meaning. Tapas flows out of deep awareness of one's limits, and restraint and absti-nence should flow naturally. Pleasure and restraint are twins, they go together. Over-indulgence is no way to enjoy life. One who practises tapas realises what is enough, what is sufficient, and is satisfied with that. Freedom from obsessive consumption is tapas.

There are four methods of self-replenishment (tapas): Humility, Service, Study and Sleep.

Humility (*vinaya*) releases one from the weight of self-importance.

Service (*sewa*) cleanses our obsession with our own problems and pre-occupations. This is not philanthropy or altruism, it is for self-renewal.

Study (*swadhaya*) of great spiritual texts and contemplation of their deep meaning is a way of self-replenishment. Chanting, singing or listening to great music is also tapas. Swadhaya literally means self-study. It is the study of the Self as well as study by yourself. This study is different from reading for information, for knowledge, for entertainment or for simply passing time. Study transforms one's life. Study of the Self is of particular importance. It is easy enough to study texts as an intellectual exercise, but that is not what is meant by swadhaya. One needs to enter into the spirit of the teachings and use the texts to reflect upon oneself and discover one's own true nature. You are your own greatest text. Know thyself! You are the microcosm of the macrocosm; when you know yourself, you know the universe. The study of a text is only a medium which may be of use to develop self-awareness; mastering the texts is not an end in itself. Equally, deeply engaging with the natural world falls within the parameters of swadhaya. Painting or contemplating a sacred painting, and any other forms of contemplative and reflective activity are self-renewing and therefore swadhaya.

Even sleeping (*nidra*) is a way of self-replenishment.

Once the Emperor of Persia asked his Sufi teacher, "What can I best do to recover and renew my soul?"

"My Lord, sleep as long as you can," came the reply.

"What do you mean? I can't neglect my duties! I have justice to deliver, ambassadors to receive, taxes to determine—so much work to do, I have no time to sleep," said the Emperor.

"But my Lord, the longer you sleep, the less you will oppress!" was the Sufi master's blunt reply.

Much of the time when we are active we oppress other people and damage the earth, which damages our souls. Therefore, sleep is a practice of tapas.

In the great Indian epic, the *Ramayana*, there is a giant called Kumbhakarna who was hyperactive. His mother prayed to Lord Shiva, "My child is too active, he can do everything in half the time, so when he has finished his work he becomes destructive; he cannot stop. So please, Lord of Lords, do something to stop him."

Lord Shiva answered her prayers, "From now on your son will only be awake for six months of the year. When he goes to sleep he will remain asleep for six months."

The modern industrial workforce is like that giant. Having completed the useful work in half the time because of technological efficiency, they cannot then stop, but go on producing the often unnecessary and wasteful goods which are destructive not only to the Earth but also to their souls. It would be a form of tapas to reduce the work time to half, say four hours a day, then the rest of the time could be given over to cultural, spiritual, contemplative and creative pursuits. And even to the tapas of sleeping!

We don't sleep enough. We watch television late into the night when we should be sleeping, and get up early in order to commute to work. That is one of the reasons we are depressed, stressed and exhausted. We have lost our common sense—we don't sleep well, we don't eat well and we work too much. The antidote to this overworked society is to recognise the value of sleeping as a spiritual practice. Sleep makes beautiful dreams possible. During dreaming the soul renews itself.

Thus the replenishment of soil, soul and society is the great work of our time. But these three should not be put into separate boxes. They should be taken together because they complement each other and complete the whole. Wholeness is implicit in this trinity.

* * *

Chapter 12

Learning from the Sun

WHEN I MET him, Vinoba was on his long walk, which would last for twenty years and which would take him to most parts of India, covering over 100,000 miles (four times the circumference of the Earth). As Mahatma Gandhi used non-violent means to bring political freedom to India, Vinoba was engaged in bringing about economic, social and spiritual freedom. He was going from village to village, addressing the landlords and persuading them to give one sixth of their land to the landless poor. Thus the spirituality of *dana* and the politics of land reform were integrated in his great journey.

"Walking is the simplest, the purest and the most natural way to travel," said Vinoba. "Your legs can reach the most remote places. Walking keeps you in touch with the earth, with people and with the state of the world. Walking is also spiritual and purifying; a form of *tapas*."

In that great walk many joined in solidarity and support. Some walked with Vinoba to be inspired and to learn. They would join him sometimes for a few days, sometimes for a few weeks. There was a party of five or six who were his permanent companions. Groups of people also went on walking missions in other parts of India to spread the idea of land gift and bring about land reform.[7]

ONE MORNING, SOON after I had joined Vinoba, we were walking alongside the Arabian Sea, north of the city of Kalicut. We started early, before dawn. As we progressed the light began to filter through. The sun was rising through the palm trees. After an hour's walking we found a beautiful coconut grove in which we took a rest. Vinoba was given a bowl of yoghurt and honey for his breakfast. All was calm, still and silent. After wiping his mouth and clearing his throat Vinoba said,

"When I am walking, some verses of the *Bhagavad Gita* come to me. I have two mothers: the one who gave me birth and the other, the *Gita*. Mother delivered me *to* the world, and the *Gita* delivered me *from* the world. Mother nourished me when I was young; the *Gita* nourished me thereafter. The *Gita* is the sweetest song I have ever heard." Then he looked up and with palms together he bowed to the sun and said:

"It is believed that the wisdom contained in the *Gita* was first given to the sun, and then to Arjuna. The sun is the perfect example of acting without desire. When the sun rises does the idea enter its mind to say 'I shall banish the darkness, I shall urge the birds to fly, and I will set people working'? No, the sun always stays still, and yet its stillness makes the world go around. If we were to thank the sun by saying, 'Your help is infinite, you have dispelled so much darkness' that would be absurd. The sun might say 'What are you talking about? Does darkness exist? Bring a little of it to show me, then I will know whether I have dispelled it. Then I shall accept that I am the doer; the maker of light.'

"The sun is totally neutral and detached," Vinoba continued. "It does not control or dictate. It just is. In the light of the sun, one person may read a fulfilling book and another a trivial one. One may help a neighbour, another may commit murder. The sun is not responsible for the good or the evil of these acts; therefore, the sun does not accumulate any consequences (*karma*). The sun would say, 'Light is my nature. For me, to be is to shine.' Even when we have night, the sun acts and shines on the other side of the Earth. The sun shines all the time, and yet no one notices that it is working. The sun sets everyone to act. It makes cows graze, birds sing, merchants open their shops, farmers plough their fields, and yet if someone does not wake up and draw the curtains, the sun will not force them to do so. It is enough that it exists. The sun is in the perfect state of *being* rather than *doing*. The sun does not *have* light; it is light. The sun does not *do* good; it is good.

"This is what Arjuna is taught in the *Gita*. Learn from the sun. Be like the sun. Just be. Be yourself, perform your *dharma*. There is a special word in the *Gita* for it—*svadharma*, which means one's own dharma. All of us have our own particular qualities (dharma) and if we are true to ourselves and live with a pure heart and without attachment, then our actions leave no residue or bondage. We accumulate no *karma*."

Vinoba stopped speaking and bowed to the sun again. After a moment I observed, "It is a natural human instinct to act with a goal in mind or for an outcome; even an unselfish or benign outcome."

"Yes," said Vinoba, "it is true. Normally when people act they desire quick and tangible results. Generally our desires are for small and insignificant achievements, so the *Gita* says to us, Give up the desire for the fruit of your action. When you give up your personal gain you will enjoy universal gains. Paradoxically, when you renounce the fruit you will gain the fruits.

"Often, people think of their self-interest, or even national interest such as Indian national interest or American national interest. To protect self-interest individuals exploit others, nations go to war, and businesses undercut each other, because people in those situations see a conflict between self-interest and the interest of others. But in reality there is no such conflict. Everyone's interests are intertwined. Peace, prosperity and happiness are in the interest of all. These are the universal gains, which are accomplished when personal gains are forgotten. When personal gains are pursued, universal gains are lost. If universal gains are lost, where are the personal gains?

"When performed with love, action becomes its own reward. When action is performed without ulterior motives, when it is spontaneous, joyful and pure, our attention is present in the here and the now. There is no cunning, there is no calculation, there is no speculation, there is no planning, there is no past, there is no future, there is no worry, there is no burden. Our action flows without stress, without strain or pressure."

What Vinoba was saying sounded good but somewhat utopian. So I asked him to give some illustrations, in order that I could grasp his point properly.

"For example," said Vinoba, "if one cooks for the joy of cooking, and with full attention and presence of mind, then good cooking will be a natural outcome. Garden for the joy of gardening, without impatience and without anxiety, then fruit, flowers and vegetables will flow from the garden of their own accord. Those who are devoted to cooking or gardening will not feel satisfied if we say to them that they need not cook or garden, we will provide ready-made meals and pre-packed vegetables. A true cook or gardener will not feel happy, because in that way they have been deprived of their creativity and joyful work.

"A gardener, while gardening with love, identifies with the vegetable kingdom. Through gardening he or she attains oneness with the whole universe. That way gardening becomes a noble act, a spiritual act, a prayer and a play—all life is a play; a divine drama. A child plays for the joy of playing; we act for the joy of acting. We should perform our actions as naturally as a bird sings. We need not expect recognition for acting according to our own nature. Gardening comes to a gardener as naturally as eating, drinking or sleeping. There is nothing special about it. There is no vanity in it."

"If there is nothing to achieve," I asked, "no goal, no outcome, then why would one act at all?"

"We cannot give up action," said Vinoba. "Action is in front of us and behind us. Even sitting still is action, and if we sit still for too long we will find even that uncomfortable. So we need not try to give up action. All we can give up is the desire for an outcome.

"Through work we express ourselves. Work manifests our imagination. Work is love made visible. Through work we establish relationships with people and material things. Thus work in itself is beautiful. It is the desire to impress others, desire for recognition, for fame and fortune, which makes work ugly. There is no need to desire any gains. All gains are by-products. The main product of work is work itself." Vinoba's discourse itself was desire-free. He was speaking from his heart. His childlike simplicity, enthusiasm and clarity of thought were mesmerising.

"But how practical is this philosophy?" I asked.

Vinoba said, "Of course we need not be oblivious of practicalities and pragmatism. For the sake of pragmatism we say, 'I will walk today to reach such and such a village by midday. In order to cover ten or fifteen miles I will begin early in the morning. Once I reach my destination I will talk to people about the value of sharing their land with the landless, and will try to persuade them to donate one sixth of the land they own.' All this planning is very practical and necessary. And yet, it can be free of the yoke of desire to succeed. The *Gita* differentiates between desire and intention. Intention leads to an attitude of gratitude (*bhavana*) which has a lightness of touch about it."[8]

This was a very inspiring morning. The sun was already above us and so we began to stride towards our destination of the day.

ON THE ONE HAND Vinoba was a sage of desireless action, and on the other hand he sought a total revolution in the social and economic structures of India which oppress the poor in grinding misery and keep the rich in isolating luxury. In his life Vinoba walked across the length and breadth of India. He collected 4 million acres of land as donations from landlords, which were distributed amongst the landless poor.

For Mahatma Gandhi, the fight for the freedom of India was selfless action (svadharma). For Vinoba, walking to bring about land reform was also a selfless act (svadharma). For them, practising spirituality in personal and political spheres dissolved the apparent duality between the inner and outer worlds. Start by serving others, and you will become self-realised. Neither Gandhi nor Vinoba divided the people into two categories—ascetics on the one hand and worldly householders on the other. The teachings of the *Gita* are intended for every man and woman as they live their daily lives in the world. Spiritual practices are for everyone. Serving people, taking care of creation, and nurturing the spirit do not demand different courses of action. Service to the world and care of the soul are one and the same thing.

*   *   *

Chapter 13

Truth is a Pathless Land

MY MEETING WITH J. Krishnamurti revealed to me a completely different approach from that of Gandhi and Vinoba. According to them, one finds meaning in life through service. But Krishnamurti emphasised the need for freedom. One needs to be free from fear and from the conditioning of the mind before any meaningful service can be performed. Inner liberty is the prerequisite of social and political liberty.

In 1960 I was in the city of Varanasi (Benares). There a friend, Achyut Patwardhan, said to me, "You must meet Krishnamurti. Your story of joining a religious order and then giving it up will intrigue him. He too gave up his Order."

I knew of Krishnamurti. Many of my friends were his fans. They were devout readers of his books and had been to his talks. But I knew very little about him giving up a religious order. Achyut eagerly dispelled my ignorance:

"Krishnamurti was born in 1895 in Madanapalle, south India. His father, a brahmin and a government employee, was a member of the Theosophical Society. After retiring from civil service the father, together with his sons, came to work and live in Chennai (Madras) at the Theosophy Centre, which was headed by the charismatic and gregarious Mrs Annie Besant. She was struck by Krishnamurti's unique aura. His deep, dark and penetrating eyes contained a kind of mystery and spirit which mesmerised Mrs Besant. She had found the 'Messiah', the world teacher, for whom she and her fellow theosophists had been waiting for so long. Mrs Besant was completely and utterly captivated by the simplicity, spirituality and purity of this extraordinary child."

Achyut stopped for a moment to take a sip of tea. I reflected that I had been nine when I met my guru. Krishnamurti was fourteen when he met Annie Besant.

"Then what happened?" I asked.

"Mrs Besant wasted no time. Over the next two years she and other theosophists formed an organisation called 'The Order of the Star in the East' and appointed Krishnamurti as its head. In 1912 they proclaimed him the world teacher, and Mrs Besant became his legal guardian and educated him in England. For the following seventeen years, until 1929, he behaved in the manner expected of him. The Order of the Star gained several thousand members all over the world, and attracted international interest. But then, after long soul-searching and going through many dark nights of confusion and angst, Krishnamurti emerged as a free spirit and renounced the role of 'an enlightened Master', 'Guru' or 'World Teacher'. He dissolved the Order and abandoned the organisation. Ever since he has been sharing his insights which have helped me and many others to seek truth and find freedom."

Achyut stopped and reached for the biscuits.

"What a story! I would be delighted to meet him. But would he have time to meet me? He must be in great demand!" I wondered.

"I will ask him, and let you know," promised Achyut.

For the entire day this story reverberated in my mind. Then in the evening around 7pm, my phone rang. I was expecting Achyut's call, and it was him.

"Yes, Satish, tomorrow at 5.30am, you and I can accompany Krishnaji on his morning walk."

"Oh, thank you, Achyut, I am thrilled. I will certainly be there." My mind was filled with anticipation that whole evening and the rest of the night. This was an entirely unexpected opportunity. I arranged a horse-driven cart (*tonga*) to pick me up. The next morning I got up at 4.30, bathed, and put on my very best *kurta* (shirt). The tonga-wallah came on time. Being so early in the morning, the streets of Varanasi were empty. I arrived at the Annie Besant school at Rajghat, where Achyut lived, and where Krishnamurti was staying. Achyut was waiting for me outside his bungalow. He said, "Namaste. Well done, on the dot."

"I wouldn't miss this opportunity for anything. Thank you for arranging it," I replied.

We walked to the guest house of the school and Achyut gently knocked on the door. It was Krishnamurti himself, ready and waiting, who opened the door.

"This is Satish, the former Jain monk," said Achyut, introducing me.

"Good morning, sir," said Krishnamurti, in a polite and soft voice. I was only an ordinary young man of twenty-four, so I was taken aback to be called 'sir'. Nobody had ever called me 'sir' before. I was speechless. Achyut led the way, Krishnamurti followed and I walked beside him, in silence. Very shortly, we were at the banks of the river Ganges. The dawn was just breaking. In that dim light I looked at the great man, about whom I had heard so much. He was sixty-five years old, yet walked at an energetic pace. Not very tall, not very large, and not self-assuming, he appeared to be a very kind man. He was looking attentively at the orange horizon on our right, beyond the holy river, as we walked north.

Just below the bank a family of pilgrims were immersing themselves in the sacred water. Beside the bathing bodies Krishnamurti saw something unpleasant, and commented, "Hindus consider the Ganges sacred, yet they let sewage, excrement and other filth of the city flow into the river. The word sacred has lost meaning and has become a mere concept. Bathing in the holy water is no more than a ritual."

There was an expression of sadness in his face. Achyut and I listened as we walked through the groves of neem and mango trees. We were silent; everything around us was still. We could hear the occasional birdsong. After we had come some distance away from the school and I felt sufficiently at ease with myself, I asked:

"Yesterday, Achyut spoke to me about you and how you dissolved the Order of the Star. You must have spoken about it many times, but I long to hear from you why you did that."

"Oh, that is a long story, and a long time ago."

"Nevertheless, that must have been such a profound and unforgettable moment," I said.

"Yes, you are right. I felt profoundly that there is no fixed programme through which truth can be delivered. Truth is a pathless land. No religion can lead us to spirituality or to freedom. Religions are as much a cause of bondage as anything. They can only offer us a religion of the prison or the cage. To walk free we have to throw away all crutches. Religions are nothing but the vested interests of organised belief, separating and dividing people. Religions are essentially based on fear. When I realised this, as clear as daylight, I said to myself: if this is so, then I cannot lead a religious order myself.

"Before I could dissolve the Order of the Star, I had to dissolve my own fear, my own insecurity. Once I did that, the rest became easier. I simply announced that the Order was not only inessential but that it was a positive barrier to true understanding, so we would have it no more. And that was that."

"That must have been a courageous step," I said. Now I felt totally relaxed. Talking while walking was very helpful.

"How did people take to your statement?"

"Obviously, there were many reactions and responses. Looking back, thirty years later, I feel that even those who took the dissolution of the Order in their stride were still looking for an ideal or an ideology, which could be an anchor and to which their minds could cling. When they realised that not only was I abandoning the Order, but I was not even putting forward an ideal for them to pursue, they were disappointed. People craved for certainty, I was offering them surprises."

"If you were not offering them an ideal, then what were you offering?" I asked.

"Friendship, conversation and dialogue, to explore the nature of reality. Truth is not a ready-made object, which can be given to you by a religion or a guru. Truth has to be discovered. Life is a journey of discovery. Certainty is only possible when there is something fixed and permanent, whereas reality is constantly moving and changing. It is constantly under-going a transformation. If our minds are tethered to a fixed belief, a certain knowledge, then how can we cope with this constant change? Since reality is not static, we need swift minds and pliable hearts. Only then can we be responsive to the dynamic nature of existence. I could not, and cannot, offer anything other than a constant conversation and exploration. Through such exploration we can enjoy total freedom from fear and from fixed ideals."

"Are you saying that there is nothing of value in great religious texts such as the *Bhagavad Gita* or the Bible?" I asked.

"There may be some value in those books as literature or as a record of someone's thinking. But truth is not in any book. If truth were there, then there would be no conflict between the Bible and the Koran, between the *Bhagavad Gita* and the Buddhist sutras. Conflict can only exist between the false and the false. There can be no conflict between the true and the true. Nor even between the true and the false. As there can be no conflict between two peace-lovers, nor between a peace-lover and a war-monger. Conflict really happens only when there are two warmongers wanting to have their way. Religious conflict is between one false religion and another false religion. Religions have become the vehicles of propaganda, and propaganda is not truth."

We were walking slowly. We came to another river, Varuna. Varanasi takes its name from two rivers: Varuna in the north and Asi in the south. These two rivers join the great Ganges, which flows on the east side of the city. As we crossed over Varuna, I said,

"Do you mean to say that religions are not part of the solution, they are part of the problem?"

"Thank you, sir," said Krishnamurti. "You have been paying attention to our conversation. You are exactly right. Truth cannot be realised through any creed, any dogma, any philosophical knowledge, any psychological technique, any ideology, any ritual or any theological system. Truth is experienced from moment to moment, in the web of relationships.

"What is the 'web of relationships'?" I asked.

"Do you realise, sir, that you are the world and the world is you? The world is not separate from you and me. There is a common thread of relationship weaving us all together. Deep down we are all totally connected. Superficially things appear separate. Separate species, separate races, separate cultures and colours, separate nationalities and religions and politics. If you look closely, you will immediately see that we are all part of a great tapestry of life. When we can see ourselves as part of this glorious pattern of relationships then conflicts between nations, religions and political systems can come to an end. Conflicts are born of ignorance. When we are ignorant of the fact that all life is interconnected, then we try to control each other. When there is no understanding that relationship is the basis of our existence, then there is only disintegration in society. Relationship is the bedrock, upon which we all stand."

We paused, then Achyut said, "This may be a good time to walk back." We must have been walking for nearly an hour. Krishnamurti was due to give his public talk at 10 am. He needed some time for breakfast and to rest before the talk. So we started to walk back. Achyut was keeping very quiet. He was happy to introduce me, a 'young rebel', to Krishnaji, an 'old rebel'.

After we turned back I asked, "You say that religion, politics and ideologies have wounded humanity. How can we heal these wounds? How can we return to the state of relatedness?"

"The problem goes much deeper than religion or politics," said Krishnamurti. "It starts in our minds, in our habits, in our lives. There is a constant conditioning which has gone on and on for centuries. We are subjected to conditioning and we participate in our own conditioning. Judging, prejudice, likes and dislikes, they are all part of the same problem. We have been conditioned to believe that the observer is separate from the observed, the thinker is separate from the thought. This dualism, this compartmentalisation, is the mother of all conflicts, basis of all pain and suffering. Do you understand me, sir? It is very important." Krishnamurti emphasised his point by closing his eyes and nodding his head vigorously.

"I hope I do. However, how do we go from dualism to wholeness?" I pursued my enquiry.

"For healing to take place, we have to go beyond theories, formulas, and ready-made answers. We have to be silent and pay attention. Silence and attention provide the ground for meditation. Meditation is a process of healing the wounds of fragmentation. In meditation, divisions end and wholeness emerges. Then there is no longer a division between 'I' and 'you', between 'us' and 'them', between 'good' and 'evil'.

"When there is no ego, no vanity, no fear, no isolation, no insecurity, no ignorance, then there is healing, and wholeness."

Being among the trees, along the water, under the sun and walking on the soft earth was itself meditative. Krishnamurti stopped; the sun was becoming warmer, and there was a presence of great beauty around. There were many more bathers in the river below. They were immersing their bodies in the water again and again, while loudly chanting Hindu mantras. They neither cared about the filth floating beside them, nor were they aware of Krishnamurti laughing explosively a few yards away.

We started to walk again. Krishnamurti asked, "What do you think, sir? What do you think?"

"It makes sense. I understand what you are saying, but looking at those bathers down below, your words seem so disconnected from the way they think, feel and live. There seems to be a big gap. What do your words mean to them?"

"Maybe nothing, nothing. And yet, unless we radically transform we may destroy not only the human race, but the Earth itself. Please think of nuclear weapons and what all that implies. A life which is whole, noble and full of clarity is an imperative for survival. It is not a utopia nor a luxury, but a necessity. Please."

Before leaving the bank of the river and turning towards the school, we stood still. Krishnamurti was looking at the sad and polluted river. There was melancholy on his face and in his voice. He said:

"Sir, what I am speaking to you is not a sentimental romanticism. Our existence, our very being, is embedded in the relationships between everything that lives and moves on Earth. This river, these trees, these animals, the singing birds, the bathing pilgrims, those leaping frogs, they are all our relations. When we look deeply and see ourselves as an integral part of the universe, then our chattering minds will calm down, the vulgarity of human warfare will vanish, we will realise a deep and abiding kinship with nature. We will never kill an animal for our appetite, we will never kill a human being to gain power."

We accompanied Krishnamurti back to the guest house and bowed to each other in parting. The moment was pregnant with deep feelings towards a new horizon for humanity.

As we approached Achyut's house, he said, "What about some breakfast? Tea and toast? Guavas and papayas? Please stay if you can."

I joined him, and together we reflected on the thoughts of

Krishnamurti. I said, "His eyes are very special. His words are radical, his thoughts are sincere, but can you ever see a time when we can be free of all temples, churches, mosques, prayers, priests, political parties, and everything else which divides humanity? Moreover, isn't he throwing the baby out with the bath water?"

Pouring hot tea into my cup, Achyut said, "We have to understand what is the baby and what is the bath water before we can assess what Krishnaji is saying. There is a difference between religion and 'the religions'. Krishnaji would agree that we need to be religious, but do we need institutionalised religions? We need the baby of the spirit, but do we need to keep the dirty water of dogmas and disciplines?"

"Krishnaji wants no ideals," I said, "but isn't he making an ideal of no ideals?"

"What is an ideal?" Achyut asked rhetorically. "An ideal is something far away, something distant, a goal, which we have to strive to achieve—if not today, tomorrow. If not in this life, then in the next. But life has to be lived now, in this moment—fully and completely. Life is here, in our friendship, in our sharing breakfast, in the digging of the garden, in being present in everything we do. This is not an ideal, even less is it an ideology, this is living."

"Achyut, you spent much of your life in politics. You were a prominent member of the Socialist Party of India. You were working to bring about a transformation through political change. But now you are living a quiet life, in this bungalow, surrounded by trees and tranquillity, while there are millions of people out there suffering. What happened?" I was full of emotion.

"More tea?" Achyut was thinking. He said, "Politics failed me; it has failed India. Politicians use the slogan of 'serving the people' as a smokescreen, as a pretext to gain power. Once they are in power their primary aim is to stay in power—by hook or by crook. I saw all this with my own eyes. The history of politics is littered with deception, corruption and delusion. So I decided that it was all a waste of time, and I got out of it. It was as simple as that. No big mystery. Politics has become, like religion, part of the problem and not part of the solution. Politics means 'divide and rule'; this was true of the British and it is true of the Congress party now. The struggle for Independence was a selfless struggle; now the struggle is for power, for privilege and for wealth."

"Then what is the alternative?" I asked.

"The alternative is in education. We must stop conditioning and corrupting our children. Therefore, Krishnamurti and his friends have started a number of schools to do exactly that: one in south India, called Rishi

Valley, another here, another in England and another in California. In these schools there are no fixed dogmas. Children are able to learn about the unity of life, about seeing things as they are, about integrity and wholeness. I find much greater satisfaction in working with children than I found in politics."

Achyut had to go to the talk by Krishnamurti, so we stopped there. But I was grateful to Achyut for making possible my encounter with Krishnamurti.[9]

Vinoba had broadened my understanding of spirituality to include service to community and to the Earth as a primary religious practice, but now Krishnamurti's search for true freedom challenged the very foundation of religious traditions.

* * *

Chapter 14

No Birth, No Death

ALTHOUGH BOTH VINOBA and Krishnamurti had talked abut the horror of nuclear weapons, it was the arrest of Bertrand Russell in England in 1961 which inspired me, together with my friend E. P. Menon, to embark upon a journey across the world. Russell had been arrested because of his protest against the nuclear bomb. If at the age of ninety he had been prepared to go to prison for the cause of peace in the world, what was I, a young man, doing? At that time there were four countries with nuclear weapons, so in solidarity with Russell we decided to walk to Moscow, Paris, London and Washington, the nuclear capitals of the world. We were blessed by Vinoba and advised by him that our walk should be undertaken without any money. After long thought and deep deliberation, we took courage in our hands and undertook to go into the unknown world like monks. We put our trust in people and the universe for our well-being.

On our long journey we faced hunger and heat, dust storms in Persia, snow storms in Russia, imprisonment in Paris, were threatened with a gun in America, and yet we also enjoyed hospitality and humour, support and encouragement, generosity and nourishment, which was offered to us spontaneously by people throughout our journey. In walking I was being true to myself (*svadharma*). Walking without desires or fixed plans enabled me to live what I had learned from Vinoba. Walking became second nature to me. I kept meditating upon the word peace (*shanti*), using it as a mantra. I was not walking *for* peace, I *was* peace. If one *is* peace, one radiates peace.

However, for our friends and family, ours was a most worrying decision. I remember the scene. We stood at the border of India and Pakistan. We were about to cross the frontier. One of my friends said, "Are you crazy? Going without money into Pakistan? Are you out of your mind? Walking into enemy territory without an escort? You are reckless. We have had three wars with Pakistan in the last twenty years! They are Muslims, they will kill you."

I said to my friend, "I understand your worries. When I start to think about it I am also apprehensive. But the most that can happen to me is death, and I am prepared for it. If I don't return alive, then I don't return alive! I have accepted it." My friend was in tears and so was I. Never before had I faced the possibility of my death in this way. In my mind I went back to my childhood. I remembered my father's death. I had become a monk to be free of death. Now I was accepting the fact that death is part of life and life is part of death.

Where there is peace there is no fear of the Other—other people, other cultures, other countries, other religions. Because peace gives us a sense that there is no Other. What separates us from others is our labels, our conditioning, our identities.

THE PROBLEM OF Hindu and Muslim antagonism has inflicted so much anguish on India and on Pakistan, but if we look at the traditional religious texts and literature, nowhere do we find such a word as Hindu. Until a few hundred years ago no concept of the Hindu religion existed. When the people from Persia, Arabia and Europe, who lived north-west of the great Sindhu or Indus river, crossed over to the south-east, they found a vast land and rich culture with tremendous diversity of faiths, philosophies and mythologies. But there was neither one God, nor one pope, nor one book. To Christians and Muslims who believed in one God and one book, this diversity was incomprehensible.

For the sake of convenience, and for the want of a better word, they described the culture and population as 'people south-east of the Indus', which became shortened to Indus, later Hindus; the land became known as India, or Hindustan, and the language was called Indi or Hindi.

Another explanation of the source of the word Hindu was once given to me by some Italians. When the Western explorers came to this part of the world they found the native people kind, generous, hospitable, helpful and deeply religious. The European travellers used a latin term to describe these people as 'in Deo' or Godly people. Hence over time it became one word, 'Indeo' and then India and Indians. That is how Columbus, encountering the peoples of Turtle Island, the Americas, and finding them free of ownership, possessiveness, selfishness and pride, named them as 'people living in God'—Indeo. Then they too were called Indians.

Some people believe that around the 14th and 15th centuries the peoples of the world were divided into two categories—Europeans and Indians. That is why words like East Indians, Red Indians and West Indies came to be used.

Whatever the truth of these suppositions and legends, my point here is that the word Hindu originally did not represent a particular religion. It was a description of people.

However, the Muslims and Christians eventually ruled the land and the people east of the Indus. In order to differentiate themselves from the local cultures and traditions they found it convenient to put everyone who was not Muslim or Christian into the category of Hindu. The constant use of this category over the centuries was so powerful that the so-called Hindus themselves accepted the label, partly because it began to suit their emerging sense of unity and relative similarity in contrast with the monotheistic 'foreign' rulers.

If the word Hindu means the people who live south-east of the Indus river, then whoever lives in that land are all people of that land. Politically and geographically, they are neither Buddhists nor Jains nor Christians nor Muslims nor even 'Hindus', but just Indians. There was never a monolithic group called Hindus. I have seen how antagonistic people can be with each other even when they are all supposed to be Hindus. In one of the towns in Kerala I had met groups worshipping Shiva and others worshipping Vishnu. They each had a separate temple. They were not on speaking terms with each other; they considered each other as enemies. Where then, was that Hindu unity? In other places I have experienced Shias and Sunnis (two Muslim sects) at loggerheads with each other. Their internal animosity was no less than their animosity towards Hindus. In Northern Ireland, Catholics and Protestants have been killing each other in the same way.

As Krishnamurti observed, religious divisions have been no less the cause of strife, violence and wars than national, political or geographical boundaries. Even if there were one world religion and one world government, there would still be conflict between factions and sects.

The Buddha was not a Buddhist, and Mahavir was not a Jain. They followed a path which led to liberation. I am as inspired by the Buddha as I am by Mahavir. For all I know, the Buddha and Mahavir may have been the same person—there are many scholars and academics who consider this probable. "Both are of royal birth; the same names recur among their relations and disciples; they were born and they died in the same country [the same district of Bihar] and at the same period of time."[10]

The Jains and Buddhists share many of the same sacred sites, and most of their teachings and techniques are also very similar. Therefore, it is conceivable that at a later period the followers of one great teacher provoked a schism and from that time one group called their founder the Buddha, the Enlightened one, and called themselves Buddhists, while the others called the teacher Jina, the Victorious one, and called themselves Jains. Later on there were further divisions among the Buddhists and also among the Jains.

AT THE BORDER of India and Pakistan I experienced a deep realisation that the Earth is a garden of Eden blessed by millions of diverse forms of life, religions, cultures, customs, costumes and colours. I wanted to celebrate this glorious diversity and embrace them all. They do not clash with, but complement each other. They all have their place. Beyond this diversity, the Earth itself is our common home and we are all bound by an undefinable human spirit and the spirit of nature.

In this book I am not going to relate the stories of my journey which brought me face to face with death as well as the most profound compassion. That story is told in my autobiography, *No Destination*. At this point I merely want to say that the journey around the world and walking across the continents released my inner spirit which was wrapped in the constraints of religious and cultural concepts. I came to the clearest conviction that we are not separate, we are all related. This realisation gave me a sense of freedom.

Now we live in an age of post-religious spirituality. The call of our time is to be a good human being rather than to be Muslim, Hindu, Buddhist, Jain or Christian. We don't have to be a special kind of person to go on the adventurous journey of the spirit. Every one of us is capable of making the hero's journey and reaching the holy grail. But to make such a journey, as Krishnamurti insisted, "we have to abandon religious dogmas and nourish the spirit."

* * *

Chapter 15

Rationalism and Non-violence

"It is undesirable to believe a proposition when there is no ground whatever for supposing it to be true."—Bertrand Russell

MY FIRST ENCOUNTER with a great Western thinker happened during my journey round the world. It was with Bertrand Russell. I admired his courage of conviction, his clarity of thought and his commitment to human well-being. Because Russell had inspired our journey on foot from India to England, it was like a pilgrimage to visit him.

My friend E. P. Menon was in correspondence with Russell, who asked his secretary Pat Pottle to bring us from London to North Wales, to the town of Penrhyn, where Russell had retired.

On one fine October evening we set off by car, heading north-west. "It is about five hours drive, depending on the traffic," said Pat, who had packed a basket full of drinks, bread, cheese, fruit, nuts and raisins to keep us nourished. Even though it was nearly the end of the 'rush hour', the traffic was still heavy, and getting out of London was slow.

"We might have some hold-up at Birmingham," said Pat, "but after that we shouldn't have any problems. Of course, the roads in Wales are winding because of the hills."

"Don't worry, Pat," I said, "this gives us plenty of time to talk." Then I asked, "Why did Russell retire to Wales?"

"First of all, Russell was born in Wales", replied Pat. "Then Wales is still such an unspoilt and quiet country—away from pollution and noise. Life is much more pleasant there, and Russell loves rural surroundings."

"What else does he love?" I asked.

"That is a very interesting question," said Pat with a broad smile on his face. After a minute's reflection, he said, "Russell loves logic, he loves peace, and of course he loves women!" This time Pat laughed loudly. "His present wife must be the fourth or fifth woman in his life, so the love of women must be very high on the list."

"He must be a man of passion," I said. "Love mixed with passion becomes very powerful. But then, passion is not so logical. How does he balance passion with logic?" I asked.

"You have touched upon what is known as 'Russell's Paradox'. Russell came to the theory of Paradox when he was working on his famous book *Principia Mathematica* which he completed in collaboration with Alfred North Whitehead," said Pat.

"That book brought Russell a great reputation," I added.

"Yes, of course," said Pat. "He got the Nobel Prize!"

"But I find his dry logic and analytic philosophy rather cold," I said.

"Many do," admitted Pat. "In fact, Russell himself used the word 'cold'. He said, 'Mathematics possesses not only truth, but supreme beauty—a beauty cold and austere like that of a sculpture.' So you are quite right."

Remembering my unease about Russell's mathematics, I said, "His love of mathematics led him to declare that all philosophy, all thoughts, even morality can be explained through mathematics. In fact Russell believes that all discoveries can be reduced to mathematical formulas. But can they?" I asked.

Pat replied, "This was the point of great disagreement between Bertrand Russell and Ludwig Wittgenstein, who believed that there are areas of thought which not only cannot be formulated in mathematical terms, but cannot even be put into words. This is his 'sphere of silence', where Wittgenstein is much closer to Eastern thought in general, and Buddhism in particular. Wittgenstein is not so much imprisoned by the cold rationality of Western philosophy. But the interesting thing about Russell is that his logic and philosophy may be cold, but his life, his actions and his politics are filled with passion."

"There are almost two personalities, even split personalities there," I said with frankness. Pat seemed to be at ease with such critical comment about his boss.

"You may be right," he said. "Look at his record in the peace movement. He was a pacifist in the first world war. He was imprisoned for being a conscientious objector, and because of his conviction he was even expelled from Trinity College, Cambridge. Then, he supported the Second World War because in his logical mind, he believed that Hitler was evil and had to be defeated." Pat continued, "A Gandhi would not do that! Russell doesn't believe that war and violence are in every circumstance a crime or inherently wrong."

"So there is inconsistency there," I said. Then I asked, "Are you saying that Russell's commitment to peace is based not on moral or ethical grounds, but on grounds of pragmatic—even mathematical—calculations?"

"I don't know," said Pat. "Even though I work closely with Russell, he is still an enigma to me, and to many others. Nevertheless, we are fortunate that a man of such giant intellect is also a champion of peace. Because of his stature he could get Einstein to sign the Peace Manifesto, which led many scientists to come together and hold the annual Pugwash conference."

"Where is Pugwash?" I asked.

"It is in Nova Scotia in Canada," said Pat. "Now the Pugwash conference is held in different parts of the world."

In between our conversations we were nibbling nuts and eating cheese. My friend E. P. Menon, himself a rationalist, said, "Whether it is on moral grounds or on pragmatic grounds, as long as we achieve peace, disarmament and justice, I am very happy. It does not matter what the motives are, what matters is the outcome."

"This is what Russell also believes," said Pat. "In CND (the Campaign for Nuclear Disarmament) Russell has worked with Christians, socialists, conservatives and many others who agree on this single issue of nuclear disarmament." All these lively conversations and the delicious food from the basket made our journey pass easily. We arrived at Penrhyn late at night, and went to bed for a long sleep so that we would be fresh and rested to see Russell the following afternoon.

He lived in a delightful but windswept country cottage near the sea. We sat in his living-room drinking tea. I could not take my eyes away from the walls of the room, as I kept looking at the impressive old paintings. Being new in the West, I did not know much about Western art, but the portraits of aristocratic figures, as well as of scientists and philosophers, were evidence of Russell's background and interests.

Russell was a slim and short man with bushy grey hair. He wore a pair of casual trousers but a crisply ironed shirt. Wearing a woollen waistcoat, a tweed jacket and a red tie, he gave the impression of an urbane intellectual entirely at ease with himself in these rural surroundings.

Though ninety-one years old, he was totally alert. His commitment to peace was unwavering and vigorous. But, as I had expected, his starting point for peace in the world was very different from my own. "I fear the end of the world. If we do not get rid of these dreadful weapons," he said forcefully, "they will get rid of us." He believed in the power of rational thought to solve the problems of war and peace and many others. He believed that there were objective and logical ways to govern and organise the affairs of the world.

"If politicians followed a rational path, a path of reason, we could create a just and peaceful society," he said. His certainty was compelling. Yet for him peace was a matter of policy, a goal to be achieved, rather than a way of life.

"A policy for peace can bring an end to the arms race," said Russell, "The choice for us in general, and for politicians in particular, is stark: either we renounce nuclear weapons or they will put an end to the human race."

"Don't you think that a change of heart is also necessary alongside a change in government policy?" I suggested. "Surely a change in policy and a change in our personal lives must occur at the same time. A policy of peace is not enough. Love of the Earth and reverence for life are the essential foundations upon which true peace can be built."

"Governments must be forced by the power of people and the power of reason to abandon the bomb," said Russell. "We cannot wait until the change of heart, that you speak of, comes about. Time is running out. A nuclear accident can cause disaster—we need to stop this madness now." Russell was adamant. He continued, "If we persist in choosing nuclear weapons, then nothing lies before us but universal death."

I was anxious to put forward a Gandhian perspective to Russell. "Maybe if people were at peace in themselves, and were prepared to live a simpler life which did not require an unlimited supply of the world's resources, there would be no need to build bombs, there would be nothing to fight over. If people did not join the armed forces, there would be no army, and if people practised right livelihood, no one would be there to work in the armaments factories. The politics of peace has to go hand in hand with the economics of peace, and a culture of peace," I said.

This meeting with Bertrand Russell was taking place at the height of the Campaign for Nuclear Disarmament (CND). There was strong opposition to the bomb, but it was concentrated on the single issue of nuclear weapons. Therefore, when I spoke about a 'culture of peace', Bertrand Russell found it idealistic, vague and impractical.

"If we make the case for peace in such broad terms," said Russell, "we are in danger of diffusing, dissipating and blunting the argument. We want to stop the nuclear arms race now; that is the only issue at stake at this moment."

After a short silence he said, "I had a frank discussion on this subject with your Prime Minister Nehru. I urged him to get the leaders of neutral countries to put pressure on nuclear powers to abandon the bomb."

Perhaps Russell was right in terms of the effectiveness of the movement.

"But nuclear weapons did not emerge from nothing," I argued. "There is a whole social and political culture behind the bomb. If you take away the bomb without questioning that culture, and the dualistic and materialistic mindset which goes with it, you will get something else equally dangerous."

This brief interview with Russell was stimulating, even if somewhat frustrating. My friend Menon and I continued to discuss these issues until late at night with Russell's secretary, in whose house we stayed.

After walking from India to Moscow, Paris and London and after meeting many ordinary people as well as political leaders, I was convinced that getting rid of the nuclear bomb was next to impossible. I felt that the nuclear countries were defending unjust and exploitative social systems. They were not going to give up their weapons, because they feared that without weapons they would not be able to maintain their power, privilege and control. Nuclear weapons were an essential part of the way these societies and governments operated.

Peace and disarmament are not possible without creating a whole culture of non-violence. In a society based on a culture of violence, the ends are considered to justify the means. Whether it is state violence, institutionalised violence, economic violence or terrorist violence, it is assumed that violence is always justified to bring about a desired order.

Violence, as well as non-violence, is a state of mind and a way of life. If we are to pick and choose which violence is justified and which is not, then there is no common culture upon which to build social, racial, religious, economic or political non-violence. In order to instigate a new culture of non-violence, it is necessary to begin at the beginning and recognise the unity and the intrinsic value of all life. A mindset which can be aggressive to nature and animals is prone to be equally aggressive to humans of other nations or religions. And that aggressive attitude to the other can translate to aggression within a national, religious or racial group.

Within India I had experienced the violence of so-called terrorist groups, who were taking up arms against the government to establish independence for their state or an equitable economic order.

If a state can justify legal violence, then terrorists can justify their violent struggle for justice. One nation's terrorist is another nation's freedom fighter. Of course, in war both sides do justify violence. All nations claim to maintain their armed forces for 'defensive' purposes. But they also believe that attack is the best form of defence: that you have to wage war to make peace.

I HAVE NEVER limited my concern to political and social non-violence. The culture of non-violence goes beyond the more rational and more humanist tradition of the West. In the consciousness of progressive groups there is a move away from the violence of nationalism, racism, sexism and religious intolerance. Yet, these groups still practise what I'd call *speciesism*, in which the human species is considered superior to all other species. The violence to non-human species often remains unnoticed. This causes grave harm to animals, forests and wildlife of all kinds. This attitude of human superiority is the foundation of the culture of violence. The dualistic mind-set which begins with controlling nature, goes on to control people. The same mindset, addicted to power, controls markets, and then builds weapons to protect those markets. If we want to be free of nuclear weapons, we have to begin at the beginning. We have to recognise the fundamental unity of all life and develop a reverence for it. Then we have to learn to live simply so that others may simply live.

If one adheres to pure rationalism, then one way or another anything can be rationalised. In Europe, rationality has been placed on the highest level, and yet the history of Europe is built on colonialism, conflicts and wars, all of which have been rationalised. European endeavours are embedded in the subjugation of people and nature. Rationalism itself is used as a weapon to destroy nature and to exploit people around the world.

European nations may have been forced to bring to an end their political colonialism—but now they are pursuing a path of economic colonialism. Scientific, technological and industrial means are the products of rationalism, which has enabled the concentration of power in the hands of Western nations so that they can establish and maintain economic control over the world.

Pure rationalism is in itself violence of the mind. Rationalism by its nature cuts through, separates, divides, isolates. This is not to say that rationality has no place in our lives. It has. But it should be kept in its place, and not given an exaggerated status in our society. Rationality tempered with the feelings and intuitions of the heart, in yin-yang balance, can create a culture of non-violence, wholeness and compassion, whereas pure Rationalism creates a culture of violence. The campaign against the bomb led by Bertrand Russell addressed the symptoms rather than the root cause. We have to ask ourselves: what kind of society do we have which can even contemplate producing and using weapons like the nuclear bomb? The bomb is only a symptom of something else. The bomb is a by-product of our blind faith in science, and the belief that all our problems can be solved by scientific methods, that the world is merely the interactions of material particles. According to Russell, even our feelings of love and fear are "but the outcome of accidental collections of atoms". How can one create a peaceful world on such a foundation? In my view, we cannot.

Unless we are able to heal the rift between science and spirituality, and develop a holistic perspective on life, peace will remain a distant dream. Science deals with what is measurable, and spirituality with what is immeasurable. Everything has these two dimensions together. How can we divide them? How can we put them into two compartments and then deny the existence of one or the other? The outer world of matter is measurable and the inner world of meaning is immeasurable, and these two aspects together form reality and existence.

Those who oppose the bomb but fail to question the fundamentals such as scientific rationalism, dualism, individualism, consumerism and materialism are never going to achieve a bomb-free future.

It is, after all, our exclusively scientific knowledge and scientific methods which split the self from the world, subject from object, mind from matter, observer from the observed, and one from the other. Science and technology embedded in a dualistic mode of thought, along with greed, fear and lust for power, are bound to give birth to the bomb and to war. Only a non-dualistic approach in which all living beings belong to a seamless web of life can free us from the bomb. This relational outlook, which is inclusive of a rational outlook, is the prerequisite for peace.

*   *   *

Chapter 16

Justice before Order

"No part of the world can be conceived in itself apart from its relation with the other parts."—Metropolitan John of Pergamon

WHILE BERTRAND RUSSELL based his vision for a peaceful world on scientific rationalism, Martin Luther King was building the American Civil Rights movement on a holistic, spiritual and non-violent foundation.

Having completed our peace march from India to Washington DC, E. P. Menon and I wrote to King asking him if he would grant us an hour of conversation. When we received his affirmative reply, we were over the moon.

We set off on a long journey to the South. The problem of black segregation and colour discrimination was present all over America, but in the South it was rampant. We were being warned by many of our friends to "be careful in the South".

THE COMFORTABLE GREYHOUND bus went from Washington to Virginia and then North Carolina, passing over many mountains and through thick forests. We stayed in Charlotte overnight, and then starting very early in the morning we travelled to South Carolina and then into Georgia.

Along the way, in small towns and large, we could see clearly how deprivation and having a black skin went together. The houses, the streets, the shops and the schools in black neighbourhoods were clearly neglected. We got off the bus and stopped at a café in a black neighbourhood of Atlanta for our lunch. Some people were playing cards, while others were chatting away. In one corner of the café some young men and women were rolling with laughter. The atmosphere in the room was informal, jolly and dignified, yet we could not help feeling that it was not the same America which we had seen during our walk from New York to Washington, especially the America of prosperous white society.

There was one middle-aged man in a red tie sitting next to our table reading a newspaper. I started to talk with him by asking directions to the town centre. Having discovered our Indian background and our plans to visit Martin Luther King, the man put his paper down and started to speak to us about the plight of the blacks.

"No good jobs, much unemployment and poor pay is one side of our problem."

"What is the other side?" I asked.

"Humiliation, injustice, disrespect and *de facto* as well as *de jure* discrimination. White people don't seem to accept that blacks are human beings too," he replied.

From this short and crisp answer it was clear that the man had a good grasp of the black predicament.

"Are you involved in the civil rights movement? Do you know Martin Luther King?" I asked.

"Yes, of course," the man replied. "I have been marching, protesting and campaigning with King for many years. He is my hero, my leader and my mentor. I know him, everybody knows him, but he may not know me."

"Then please tell us more about King," I asked.

"Yes, with pleasure. What do you want to know?"

"Anything you can tell us. It would be good to know his background before we meet him," said E. P. Menon.

"There are lots of articles and books about King you should read! He is our local hero first and foremost. We love him because he was born (in 1929) and brought up here in Atlanta itself. His father as well as his grandfather were pastors in a Baptist church. The priesthood runs in his family, I suppose. King followed in the footsteps of his father and grandfather and became a pastor himself. Being a church minister, he had good training for public speaking. I also think that he has a special gift for oratory. He is a born orator. You should have heard him speak at the march on Washington (28th August 1963) when he gave that famous 'I have a dream' speech. I was there. God spoke through King—he was electrifying. A quarter of a million people were there in front of the Lincoln memorial, and yet there was a pin-drop silence when he spoke. King was charismatic, mesmerising, inspiring and reassuring. Passion, wisdom and uncompromising radicalism were the hallmarks of that speech. We loved it and we loved him. That day every black man, woman and child was proud of him. The audience was ecstatic. That march and that speech marked a turning point for the civil rights movement. Now we are on a winning path." Obviously the man was full of enthusiasm, commitment and dedication for the liberation of black America.

"How did King become involved in the civil rights movement in the first place?" I asked.

"Don't you know the Montgomery bus boycott?" the man asked us, with some surprise on his face. He could not believe that we could be so ignorant, and yet be going to meet Martin Luther King. "You should have done your homework," he said in exasperation.

With apology in my voice, I said, "In fact we have read the story in the newspaper articles but we want to hear it from the mouth of a black activist like you to refresh our memories, if you don't mind."

The man was very kind. He said, "I have to rush off soon as I'm going to a civil rights meeting to plan our future campaigns, but briefly speaking it was a woman called Rosa Parks who started it all. In the town of Montgomery, in December 1955, Rosa got into a bus. All the buses of the town had two sections; front for the whites and back for the negroes. In the back section there was one seat free, and Rosa settled there. The ridiculous rule of the bus system was not only to have 'whites only' and 'blacks only' sections, but if all the seats of the 'whites only' section were full and a white person got on the bus, then a black person should give up his or her seat. How much more unjust can you get?" the man emphasised the point loudly.

"Then what happened?" I asked.

"A white man got on the bus but there was no free seat for him, so the white male bus driver asked Rosa to stand up and give her seat to the white man! Can you believe it?" The man was obviously enjoying telling us the story.

"And Rosa Parks did not stand up?!" I interjected.

"Of course not," said the man. "Rosa said she was very tired and she was not going to give up her seat. Hearing this, all the fellow black passengers were stunned in admiration of Rosa's courageous response. When the driver physically forced Rosa off the bus every single black passenger followed her. The driver was surprised at their solidarity and defiance."

I knew that the man had to go soon, but we wanted him to continue the story, so my friend E. P. asked, "Is that how the famous bus boycott began?"

"Yes," said the man. "Then and there on the pavement itself Rosa asked, 'How long are we going to put up with this humiliation? Let us never ride in these buses unless and until the rules change and every passenger buying the same ticket receives the same treatment, and let us spread the word today, this evening, around the entire black neighbourhood. Whatever happens I am never going to ride in these buses of discrimination and disgust.'"

"Did everybody agree to her suggestion?" I asked.

"Yes, they did," the man answered, "and the word got around throughout the community very fast. Everybody said, 'Enough is enough; we will all walk.'"

"How did Martin Luther King come into this picture?" I asked.

"King at that time was the pastor of the local church. He not only gave his support, he actively organised the car-pooling and fund-raising for taxis, and led the campaign to end bus discrimination. Rosa Parks and Martin Luther King became the two great heroes of the movement."

"How long did the boycott last?" I asked.

"For 381 days. Thousands of black people walked to work, walked to the shop, walked to the church, walked to schools, walked to hospitals, walked everywhere. It was a walking revolution. People sang religious and revolutionary songs as they walked. Most of the city buses stood idle as the black passengers were the majority of their customers. Never in the history of America had such a joyful, non-violent protest been witnessed. The authorities, media and the general public could not believe that the black people were capable of such orderly and determined protest."

"Amazing story. Then how did it end?" I asked.

"The black people lost their case in the local courts," the man answered, "but they won in the Supreme Court and of course, in the court of public opinion. When the bus discrimination was declared unconstitutional, interestingly, the same driver who had ejected Rosa Parks from his bus welcomed her in the desegregated bus. It was a true reconciliation, a real example of peaceful conflict resolution and a victory for non-violent action."

"But that was only one victory," I suggested. "The colour discrimination in general still continues."

"The prejudices of centuries cannot be dispelled overnight. But that victory gave us hope and confidence. Martin Luther King and many of us were radicalised. King went to jail. So did many others. Our struggle continues," the man said calmly.

"But," I said, "there are many young militants who feel that justice postponed is justice denied. The way of non-violence for them is too slow. Some of the Freedom Rides organised by the revolutionary students have resulted in violence. Also people like Malcolm X and Stokeley Carmichael and other Black Power leaders are on a different wavelength from King. What do you think of them?"

"They have a point," said the man with a broad smile, "but only to a limited extent. You must put these questions to Mr King himself. I'm sorry, I'm getting late, I must go."

We too set off on the last stretch of our journey, and soon arrived at the offices of the Southern Christian Leadership Conference, of which King was the President. We were greeted by a young woman in reception wearing casual clothes. Her skilfully plaited hairstyle attracted my attention. She guided us into the small and simply arranged office of Martin Luther

King. And there we were. King received us with a gracious smile. In his blue suit, white shirt and blue tie, he looked rather formal and formidable, but his manners and expression were most gentle and friendly. We were facing the *Time Magazine* Man of the Year, and the winner of the Nobel Peace Prize. For a few seconds I felt intimidated in his presence, but King was quick to engage us in conversation and make us feel at ease.

"I'm amazed that you have walked all the way from India and without any money," King said. "How do you eat? How do you live? Do you beg for food and shelter?"

"We are walking as peace pilgrims," I said, "As pilgrims we practise patience. We have learnt to wait until help or a gift is offered to us, and then to take less than what is offered."

"How do you do that?" King asked.

"When we arrive in a strange place we begin to make contact with people whom we have never met before by giving what we can give, rather than by asking. We give them our presence, our stories, our songs, and we take genuine interest in their lives. When people are engaged they begin to ask questions and find out who we are and why we are walking, and why we carry no money. Once they discover the nature of our journey, in most cases they start to open up and show their generosity. After walking through a dozen countries for over two years we have found that people are people everywhere. The natural instinct of people in all countries, cultures and religions is to be helpful. Hospitality is normal, hostility is exceptional."

"Have you developed some techniques to dissolve people's suspicion of strangers?" King was curious.

"There is no fixed technique. Pilgrimage is a creative process. Every situation is different. Every day is a new day. Trust is the foundation, the ultimate and perhaps the only technique. We never have such doubt in our hearts that one day we might not get any help offered to us," I said.

"But there must have been occasions when no help was offered. What did you do then?" King probed further.

"That too was a good day; an opportunity to fast, an opportunity to sleep under the stars. In a sacred journey, an opportunity to suffer is as much a gift as an opportunity to celebrate. No situation is constant, everything passes," I said. After a moment's pause I continued, "But we have come to ask you some questions and seek your guidance. We want to know your views about peace and how it can be promoted."

"Strong and wealthy governments are engaged in an arms race. They want to outdo each other in inventing, producing or acquiring better, faster and more lethal weapons. This race can only end in disaster." Then, pointing to the picture of Mahatma Gandhi, which was hanging on the right-hand side of the wall, King continued, "As he warned, 'An eye for an eye makes the whole world blind.' So instead of an arms race, I urge countries to engage in a peace race. Let all nations compete with each other in inventing better, faster and more efficient means of making peace."

"How can we move from an arms race to a peace race?" E. P. Menon asked.

"By reordering our priorities," King answered. "America, being the richest and most powerful country, should set an example and show the way. Pursuit of peace should take precedence over pursuit of war." King's answer was simple, clear and straightforward. "It is not rocket science to realise that in peace lies true security. Settling differences through war, through burning human beings with bombs and filling homes with orphans and widows, is no way to conduct human affairs. We may have guided missiles but we have misguided politicians."

"In our encounters with politicians around the world," I said, "we have found them saying 'We are for peace; it is the other side provoking war.'"

"It is a feeble blame game," retorted King. "In the nuclear age, the threat of annihilation is such that we have to choose between non-violence and non-existence. The challenge of nuclear weapons is such that either we must learn to live together as brothers and sisters, or we are all going to perish together as fools."

"You mentioned non-violence. Do you consider peace and non-violence as interchangeable?" I asked.

"True peace is not merely the absence of war," said King. "It is the presence of justice, equity and a non-violent social order. Non-violence is a moral force which can transform individuals and societies and bring peace. Thus peace and non-violence are twins."

"What are the outstanding attributes of non-violence?"

"The method of non-violence seeks neither to humiliate, nor to defeat the opponent, or the oppressor, or the so-called enemy. Non-violence seeks to win friendship and understanding which leads to reconciliation. In this way no one loses, both sides win. Non-violence is as much about the liberation of the oppressor as it is about the liberation of the oppressed."

"Some of your black activists consider non-violence a sign of weakness," I said.

"But it is not," said King. "If I hit you, you hit me back, then I hit you back. That can go on *ad infinitum*. Only a strong and brave person can break the chain of hate. A great moral strength is required to follow the discipline and dignity of love. Non-violence is neither passivity nor surrender to injustice. The means of non-violence are better for achieving transformation because they produce no negative side effects. That is why I insist on non-violence in our struggle for civil rights."

"What is the biggest stumbling block in your struggle?" I asked.

"It is not the Ku Klux Klan or other obvious racist groups, as generally might be assumed. In my view it is the moderate white society which prefers order over justice. They prefer the negative peace of sweeping the tension under the carpet, rather than facing the facts and dealing with the horrors inflicted upon the black people. Injustice to us here is injustice everywhere. For the oppressed, liberation is an urgent need. Sweet words of peace, order and harmony hide the reality of entrenched racism. The white liberals want order today and justice tomorrow, which never comes. We want justice today and order will be a natural outcome. Justice will produce order, not the other way around." After a few moments of silence, King said jokingly, "We want to be the white people's brothers, not brothers-in-law."

"The liberals want gradual change," I commented.

"Gradual yes, but the change must start now and it must be visible. If America continues to judge some of her children not by the strength and content of their character but by the colour of their skin, then those children are not going to sit quietly and be orderly. They are going to rebel, riot and break the laws. A riot is, ultimately, the cry of the unheard. There comes a time when the oppressed can bear it no more. In fact, when faced with injustice, keeping silence and submitting to the forces of law and order is a betrayal of love. Non-violence is not silence; it is better to die for justice rather than submit to an unjust order."

Concerned that he might be misunderstood, King continued further, "I advocate non-violent rebellion. Let no-one, not even white racists, pull us so low as to hate them. We should love our opponents and yet we should stand up for justice. This is a fine balance. This is the core of Christian teachings, and Mahatma Gandhi proved it possible during his struggle for the independence of India. We are doing the same. We are proving that justice can be brought about with the means of love and non-violence."

Suddenly the door opened behind us. There was the young woman with her beautiful hair plaits from reception, who indicated that King had to go to another meeting. We had to bring an abrupt end to our conversation, but were more than delighted to have bathed in this extraordinary man's wisdom.

*   *   *

Chapter 17

Poverty and Progress

"Even as a child I felt terror-struck when I heard it said that to live an agreeable life you have got to be rich."—Berthold Brecht

I FIRST MET E. F. Schumacher in 1968. He was as radical a contrast to Bertrand Russell as was Martin Luther King. I had read Schumacher's essay on 'Buddhist Economics' and I thought: here is a voice of wisdom and reason united. The essay made me realise that holistic thought was not the preserve of the East, nor was rational thinking the preserve of the West. Being with Fritz Schumacher felt like being in the presence of an Eastern sage like Vinoba or Gandhi, and yet Schumacher was deeply imbedded in the Western intellectual tradition.

Comparing Schumacher with Mr Nehru, the first Indian prime minister, it became clear to me that Nehru was ideologically much closer to the Western rationalism of Bertrand Russell. Nehru accepted Gandhi's leadership because it suited him in the particular circumstances of India's struggle for independence; but he accepted non-violence only as a tactic to overthrow the British Raj. As soon as he came to power he opted for the industrialisation and militarisation of India along Western lines. Forgetting the Gandhian ideals of peace, simplicity and a non-violent social order, he saw the Indian villagers, farmers and artisans as uneducated members of a backward class, and the Western model as 'development'.

Nehru's project was to 'civilise' India. Because he had a greater empathy with the rationalist and technological paradigm, civilisation and Westernisation were synonymous to him. The only future for India, according to Nehru, was to catch up with Western living standards. An India without cars, without jets, without steel and big dams was an 'undeveloped' country. Heavy industry and huge dams were his 'new temples'. They were the symbols of progress. As a consequence, the religious temples became symbols of backwardness and superstition.

Never mind the great Indian culture, literature and architecture; never mind the mythology, philosophy and music; never mind the great tradition of craftsmanship and farming. All these were insignificant. What mattered was air-conditioning, refrigerators, telecommunications and mass production of consumer goods. Gandhi said to Nehru, let us have production by the masses rather than mass production. India is a country of masses. Industrialisation, mechanisation and automation will render millions of hands idle. Why not use human energy instead of petroleum? Why seek electric power and abandon muscle power? Nehru remained unconvinced. After Independence, Gandhi was assassinated and Nehru was in a position to lead India along the path of Westernisation.

Following the second world war, at the United Nations, American President Truman redefined the world in terms of the 'developed' and the 'undeveloped'. Much of the white world he defined as 'developed', while much of the coloured world as 'undeveloped'. So at a stroke a new concept came into being; the word development took on a new meaning. It was now used purely in terms of an industrial economy. All manner of production must be industrialised: food, clothes, housing, and everything else. The economies of artisans, peasants, small farmers and traders were made retrograde, inefficient, uneconomic, irrelevant, out-of-date, and a cause of poverty. Economic growth became the new 'god'. Economies of scale became the new 'religion'. Development agencies became the 'missionaries' of materialism.

This notion of development was presented with many promises: the removal of poverty, alongside high living standards, comfort and convenience, unlimited leisure, reduction of working hours, unlimited mobility, entertainment, opportunity and fun, were the carrots. The threat of being left behind and excluded from the high table of Western leaders was the stick. Most of the government leaders and industrialists of the non-white world, like Prime Minister Nehru, were seduced. The promises were too glamorous to resist, the threats were too dangerous to risk.

BUT FRITZ SCHUMACHER, despite being a Western economist, stood against this view of development. His ideal of a holistic, decentralised and local economy was encapsulated in the dictum 'Small is Beautiful'. He pointed out the utter failure of the development paradigm to fulfil its promises. Within a few decades it became clear that all the development projects were in reality of most benefit to Western countries, and to a lesser extent to the elite of the so-called developing countries. The industrial economic model was very expensive, very wasteful, very polluting and totally unhelpful to the poor. Development was destroying the traditional way of life as well as the livelihoods of the majority of people.

When it started, industrialisation in the West had also primarily bene-fited the privileged and the rich, while the poor suffered and the working class was created; and many small farmers lost their livelihoods. The living standards of the poor in the West rose only when Western countries started to use the cheap labour of the non-white world, and imported cheap raw materials, cheap food, and cheaply manufactured consumer goods. They also made use of the 'undeveloped' world as a market for the sale of their own products and manufactured goods, such as clothes, cars, tractors, tele-vision sets, tobacco, Coca-Cola, pesticides, fertilisers, and more shamefully, armaments. The net flow of wealth flows from the poor to the rich coun-tries. Even the end of political colonialism did not change that fact. If any-thing, the modern free-market economy has intensified it and thus created a new economic colonialism.

In his book *Small is Beautiful*, Schumacher brought these facts to the attention of the world. The market economy was not only impoverishing the poorer countries but destroying the soul of Western society and under-mining the quality of life everywhere. Free trade was not only a free raid on the poor, it was also damaging the integrity and morality of its perpetrators.

Schumacher called for the adoption of 'Buddhist Economics' because he believed that economics without ethics, without morality, without spir-itual values, was like sex without love. Pursuit of wealth for its own sake and for the sake of physical gratification is nothing but a form of prostitu-tion. The obsession with comfort is bringing moral bankruptcy to Western society, while devastating traditional cultures and natural environments.

Schumacher questioned the way the meanings of 'wealth' and 'poverty' have been distorted by the advocates of economic growth. The meaning of wealth has been reduced to the accumulation of money and material goods, while a rich family life, a rich community, the abundant wealth of natural beauty, time for friendship, contemplation and celebration, are all sacrificed for financial gain. "A society suffering from spiritual poverty yet considering itself as wealthy is the ultimate delusion," said Schumacher.

SIMILARLY, THE MEANING of poverty has also been distorted. Poverty is not to be equated with misery or starvation. Originally, poverty meant the vol-untary acceptance of a materially simple and uncomplicated life and the renunciation of unnecessary possessions. In the Christian tradition a monk takes the vow of poverty, which means that simplicity should underpin the religious life. The first beatitude in the Sermon on the Mount is, "Blessed are the poor, for theirs is the kingdom of heaven." Furthermore, Jesus says, "It is easier for a camel to go through the eye of a needle than for a rich man to enter into the kingdom of God."[11]

St Francis, the son of a wealthy merchant, left his material possessions to abide with 'Lady Poverty'. The Buddha, son of a wealthy king, did the same. He gave up his palace, his horses, his elephants, his pomp and his crown, and took a begging bowl to seek enlightenment. Mahavir, also a prince, gave up the royal life.

In our own time, Shakers sang the hymn 'It's a gift to be simple, it's a gift to be free.' Their culture of elegant simplicity gives the sense of incomparable aesthetic pleasure and brings freedom to the soul.

Mahatma Gandhi renounced his barrister's suit in favour of a loincloth. Once visiting London to meet the King he was asked by a journalist, "Aren't you going to dress more suitably for your audience with the King?" To which Gandhi replied, "Don't worry, the King will be wearing enough clothes for both of us!" Churchill denigratingly called him a 'half-naked fakir', yet he was revered by millions.

Western rationalists have an entrenched habit of classification. They have classified the world into developed and undeveloped, the rich and the poor, civilised and uncivilised, educated and uneducated, and so on. If the classification was for the sake of understanding alone that would be one thing, but it is used to put one class above the other; so being rich is better than being poor, being developed is better than being undeveloped. The rich and the developed then take it upon themselves to make a mission of forcing everybody to follow their example—their monoculture—and to make the poor feel inadequate when they are not like the rich.

For millennia there have been peoples all over the world who lived in great simplicity without ever considering themselves 'poor', 'undeveloped' or 'uncivilised'. My own family in Rajasthan lived without the trappings and trivia of what is considered to be rich and advanced, and yet we never thought of ourselves as 'poor'. We were who we were—human 'Beings', not human 'Havings'!

Many tribal cultures and peasant societies lived and still live without war, without corruption, without pollution, without nuclear weapons, without population explosions, without exploitation, without drug abuse. And yet we call them poor and uncivilised, in need of 'development'. The Western ideology of materialism is teaching them to consider themselves poor and making them struggle to become rich. The rich show images, through advertising, which make people feel inferior, inadequate and deprived. It is like an unwritten conspiracy to undermine simple, agrarian and traditional local cultures and their economies.

'Only the rich can have a good life' is the dominant ideology that has been drummed into the ears of most societies. Development and progress are judged according to the increase in disposable income. Countries are competing with each other to raise the average income per head of their citizens. Increase of money supply has become the be-all and end-all of development activities.

Schumacher made a distinction between ephemeral wealth and eternal wealth. Ephemeral wealth is limited to the standard of living, whereas eternal wealth is about the quality of life. Schumacher wrote:

"In the former, there may be opulent living in terms of ephemeral goods, and starvation in terms of eternal goods—eating, drinking and wallowing in entertainment, in sordid, ugly, mean and unhealthy surroundings; while in the latter there may be frugal living in terms of ephemeral goods and opulence in terms of eternal goods—modest, simple and healthy consumption in a noble setting. . . . The lifestyle of modern industrial society is one that places primary emphasis on ephemeral satisfactions and is characterised by a gross neglect of eternal goods. . . . Many pre industrial societies have been able to create superlative cultures by placing their emphasis in exactly the opposite way.

"The affluent societies of today make such exorbitant demands on the world's resources, create ecological dangers of such intensity, and produce such a high level of neurosis among their populations, that they cannot possibly serve as a model to be imitated by those two-thirds or three-quarters of humankind who are conventionally considered underdeveloped or developing. The *failure of modern affluence*—which seems obvious enough, although it is by no means freely admitted by people of a purely materialistic outlook—cannot be attributed to affluence as such, but is directly due to mistaken priorities. A gross overemphasis on the ephemeral and a brutal undervaluation of the eternal. Not surprisingly, no amount of indulgence on the ephemeral side can compensate for starvation on the eternal side."[12]

Schumacher advocated a culture of simplicity based on his knowledge that the real needs of human beings are limited. They must be and can be met. But their greed and wants are unlimited—they cannot be met. The rich are chasing their wants and the poor are trying to meet their needs.

In the context of Schumacherian thinking, poverty is not the problem; affluence is the problem and poverty the solution. The problem is not poverty, it is social injustice, human exploitation, conspicuous consumption and the loot of the natural world. And these are perpetuated by the rich, not by the poor. People with wealth have diverted our attention—they always talk about the poor as if they are the problem. In the name of aid and development a few crumbs are thrown at the poor, so that the rich can salve their consciences and feel that they are doing their bit, and also keep the poor from revolting. At the same time the rich go on amassing more and more wealth and power for themselves. It is now important to change the focus. Instead of aid, and pretending to be 'giving' to the poor, the wealthy classes and countries should take less from the poor. Let the poor keep their land, their crafts, their local economies, their indigenous cultures, their modest access to forests and fishing.

Our attitude towards the poor needs radical change. The moment our attitude changes, everything will start to change. Right attitude will produce right relationship and also right language.

If our focus is on affluence, on accumulating more and more possessions and on thinking that being rich is a status symbol, such a mindset will corrupt our actions and our lives. But if the focus is on creativity, on human relationships, on beauty and aesthetics, on arts and culture, on community and spirituality, then money is of lesser importance.

The poor work hard. They have sufficient knowledge to grow their food, build their homes, weave their clothes, stitch their shoes and make their tools, but the rich and powerful have grabbed all the resources. They own the land. They own the forests and fisheries. Instead of giving aid the rich should stop preventing the poor from accessing the sources of subsistence. Instead of complicated, expensive and sophisticated technology let the rich respect the simple technologies of the poor.

Schumacher called these 'intermediate' or 'appropriate' technologies.

The elite come up with their high-tech solutions, then they impose these technologies upon the poor. Those who cannot afford to buy them find that the old tools and technologies upon which their livelihoods depend have been undermined. Making things by hand either becomes a luxury or falls into oblivion.

"But where do you begin the process of transformation?" I once asked Fritz. "How does change come about?"

"It has to begin with a change of heart and a change of attitudes. At present our emphasis is on 'the economy' and ephemeral wealth. The eternal values are secondary. This needs to be the other way around." To illustrate this point Fritz related a story.

"Once there were two monks. Both of them were smokers. One day they were talking about their habit of smoking. They said, we are monks and we should be in prayer all day long. Is it possible for us to meditate and smoke at the same time? They could not resolve the riddle. They decided to consult their abbot. The first monk went to see him, asked his question and came out of the abbot's room. Then the second monk did the same. Later on the two monks met again, and talked about what had been said. The second monk asked the first monk, "What did the abbot say?"

The monk replied, "Oh, the abbot said, 'No, no, never. Never do it.' "

"I see. That is strange."

"Why?" said the first monk, "What did he say to you then?"

"He said, 'Yes, that's fine, carry on, carry on, carry on. Any time.' "

"How is that possible, two answers to the same question?"

Then the second monk asked the first, "What did you ask?"

"I asked, 'Can I smoke while I am praying and meditating?', and the abbot said, 'No, no, never, don't do it.' "

The first monk asked the second, "What did you ask?"

"I asked, 'Can I pray and meditate while I am smoking?', and the abbot replied, 'Carry on, carry on, carry on. Any time!' "

Fritz explained, "Eternal values are equal to prayer and meditation. If we get distracted by money and material things, we are like the first monk whose meditation is interrupted by the smoking. Because in this case smoking is primary and meditation is secondary. But if we seek spiritual meaning while earning our living then we are like the second monk, able to transcend the ephemeral and experience the eternal, because in this case meditation takes over from smoking."

IN 1975 I WAS to return to India. Having spent four years in the West I felt that it was time for me to return to my roots. I was missing India. Sweet mangoes and soft papayas, warm winters and cool rains, high Himalayas and fertile plains were calling me.

I spoke to my friend Fritz about my plans to leave England. He was dismayed. We had become very close over the last few years. I often used to visit him at his home in Caterham, and join him in grinding the week's wheat flour in his Samap hand mill. We engaged in lengthy conversations while the bread was rising and baking in the oven. In the afternoons when the sun was shining, we would weed the garden, make compost or plant out seedlings. At other times we would simply go for a walk. Many thoughts on ecology, spirituality, organic farming, holistic philosophy were the content of our wide-ranging and endless conversations.

"Look, Satish, there are many Gandhians in India, but very few in England. So you'd better stay here. Nobody is going to miss you in India!"

Obviously Fritz did not like the idea of my giving up the editorship of *Resurgence* and retreating to India.

"Moreover, you bring a particular flavour to *Resurgence* which makes it unique—a blend of East and West. If it were edited by an English person, it might become like any other magazine. So why not stay?"

At about the same time Mrs Indira Gandhi declared a State of Emergency in India. Many radical Gandhians such as J. P. Narayan and Siddharaj Dhadda were imprisoned. It was likely, I was told, that because of my close association with them, I might also be thrown into jail. My friends in India wrote suggesting that instead of returning I should stay in England and campaign from there for the restoration of democracy in India.

I thought long and hard, and in the end took Fritz's advice and remained in the UK. But from time to time I kept returning to India for spiritual nourishment, social engagement and ecological insights. In the next part of the book I will describe some of my travels and encounters, disappointments and inspirations experienced in India.

* * *

PART THREE

Travels
in India

*Tongues in trees . . . sermons in stones,
and good in every thing.*
—William Shakespeare

And the time will come
when you see we're all one
and life flows on
within you and without you.

—George Harrison

Chapter 18

Islam, a Religion of Peace

"WHAT IS THE ESSENCE of Islam?" I asked a great Muslim thinker, Maulana Wahiduddin Khan, during a visit to New Delhi.

"Let me answer your question by relating an episode from the life of our Prophet. One day a man came to him and said 'I am a very simple person. I don't understand theology or philosophy. But I wish to follow your teachings. Please tell me one simple truth by which I can order all the affairs in my life.'

"The prophet answered, 'Avoid being angry at all times'.

"This answers your question.

"Islam is not about theories or philosophies, it is about living. By not being angry at all times we can serve God and people and obtain peace of mind. It is not enough to be peaceful when the circumstances are favourable to peace. The prophet taught us that we should remain peaceful at all times. We should not get angry even when provoked, even when someone abuses us, even when someone disagrees with us and even when someone commits an act which we consider to be wrong."

Maulana Wahiduddin Khan lives near the impressive and spacious tomb of Nizamuddin in New Delhi. His house is guarded by police because his kind of teaching is not popular with some of his fellow Muslims. He has received death threats. So I commented, "But many Muslims don't agree with you."

"No, they don't," the Maulana said. "It is part of human nature to have different points of views, different perspectives, different ideas, different beliefs and different religions. Nevertheless, I believe all those differences should be respected. And if those differences give birth to conflict and disputes—whether family disputes, religious disputes, national disputes or international disputes—then those disputes should be resolved only by dialogue and by peaceful means. Islam means 'in peace'. For us, peace is paramount. When we meet someone we greet each other by saying 'Peace be with you'. So peace is the essence of Islam."

"Then what about the concept of *jihad,* holy war?" I asked. "How can peace and holy war coexist in Islam?"

The Maulana paused for a second. Stroking his long beard he looked into my eyes. Then he spoke calmly,

"Well, the meaning of jihad has been grossly misunderstood. I don't understand why even my fellow Muslims distort the meaning of this word. Many learned and intelligent people have misinterpreted that word. As I said to you just now, the very meaning of 'Islam' is peace, so how can we ever contemplate war? Any kind of war? How can we teach peace and war in the same breath?

"You are a Jain. You well know what the word Jain means. It means victorious. The founder of the Jain religion was Mahavir, which means Great Warrior. No religion has put so much emphasis on non-violence and peace as the Jains, and yet they use the language of warriorship and victory. Victory over whom? Who is our enemy? Lust, greed and selfishness are our enemies. The victory is victory over these hidden enemies within. Jihad does not mean war, it means struggle. What is our struggle? Our first and foremost struggle is to fight against our ego and overcome our pride. We must defeat the forces of anger. That is jihad. Then we must struggle against injustice, against the exploitation of the weak by the strong. Yet, all struggle must be non-violent. There is no place for any kind of violence in Islam."

"But the Prophet was a great general and led armies," I commented.

"Yes, but in those days battles were fought with bows and arrows. There were no weapons of mass destruction. Now times have changed: we are living in a new context, the context of the nuclear age. Now soldiers don't fight wars, they drop bombs from high above. Uncounted numbers of innocent civilians are killed, whereas hardly any soldiers are involved in the air bombardment of modern times. Therefore, we cannot go back to the times of the Prophet. We have to bring the Prophet to our time, and imagine what the Prophet would say to us now. I believe that he would speak of non-violent methods of struggle. Nowadays governments can be elected or defeated by people; therefore, we can use democratic means to bring about change."

"But in practice, there seems to be less emphasis on non-violence amongst Muslims," I observed.

"Yes, that is true, but do not judge Islam by Muslims, judge Muslims by Islam. There are fifty-seven countries claiming to be Islamic, but in my view not one of them is truly practising Islam. This is tragic. But then, could we not say the same of Christian countries? The number of wars fought by Christians in Europe, and violent acts perpetrated by them in other continents makes sad reading. What does it mean? It only means that Christians are not practising the teachings of Christ, who said, 'Love your neighbour as yourself.' He went even further and said, 'Love your enemy and turn the other cheek.' Tell me how many Christian countries are practising this? The United States of America is supposed to be a country full of Christians, and yet that country is spending so much money, using so many resources of the Earth on armaments. If those resources were used wisely, America could help to bring an end to hunger, disease and deprivation all over the world. But the USA seems to prefer spending resources on weapons of mass destruction rather than on the well-being of the Earth. Will you blame Christianity for that?"

"No, but so often religions seem to cause violence," I said.

"It saddens me that we live in a culture of violence," said the Maulana. Politicians use religious differences to their selfish advantage. They don't realise that such advantages in the end turn into greater disadvantage. It is beyond me why politicians seem to believe that only by dividing can they rule. Why not rule by uniting? Particularly in India we need to bring a sense of unity between the Hindus and Muslims. We may have two religions, but we are the same people. We have much more in common than we realise. There is more to unite us than to divide us. Our destiny is the same. Now and for ever we have to share the same land. We will always be neighbours."

"Then what do you say to your fellow Muslims in India?" I asked.

"I say to them that it is a matter for celebration that India has embraced a secular constitution; secular does not mean 'non-religious', rather it means 'all religions'. Let a thousand flowers bloom. We need not pick a fight with the Hindus. They are our brothers and sisters. We need them. We must travel together. We must identify ourselves with India, it is our country, it is our home, and we must play our full role in the affairs of India."

"But some Muslims in Kashmir wish to separate themselves from India, either to become part of Pakistan or to become independent. What is your view on that?" I asked.

"That has nothing to do with Islam really. This is politics. Religion is being misused here; it is neither spirituality nor religion. Politics divides, spirituality unites. In any case, even in political terms, if one hundred and forty million Muslims in the rest of India can be content, then why is there a problem for the Muslims of Kashmir to live in India? And if the Muslims of Kashmir cannot live in India, then wouldn't the Hindus say, 'Why should the rest of the Muslims be in India?' The separatists are weakening and undermining the status of Indian Muslims. Therefore the question of Kashmir should not be viewed as a Hindu-Muslim question.

"If the people of Kashmir want more autonomy, more local decisions, more self-determination, that is fine. That should be handled politically, not religiously. It may be that all the states of India—and of Pakistan, for that matter—should have more local autonomy. For example Mahatma Gandhi was in favour of a much more decentralised political structure than what we have now. That ideal could be pursued in its own right. Why bring religion into this equation? Religion is to enhance the community spirit and to nurture unity. Religion is to find who we are. A religion is no religion if it cannot teach us how to tap our own inner source of peace. We can go on looking for peace in politics, in materialism, in sectarianism. I tell you, we will only find frustration and exhaustion.

"There is a story about a musk deer, who has musk in his belly button. The deer smells the musk. It is a delicious smell, and the deer wonders, where does this smell come from? He wants to find the source of this wonderful fragrance. He runs to the east and doesn't find it. He runs to the west, to north and south, and still doesn't find it. He runs and runs but cannot reach the source of the smell. Finally, exhausted and exasperated, he falls down. He curls up, his nose comes closer to his belly, and there he smells the sweet smell of musk, and sighs with relief and joy.

"We need not run around the world to find our peace, our dignity, our freedom. It is within us. Muslims need not look for peace through political structures. We should understand that peace is a state of mind, a way of being. That experience of peace is rooted within us."

MAULANA WAHIDUDDIN IS a Sufi. Like the Celts among Christians, the Kabbalists among the Jews, and the Bhaktas among the Hindus, the Sufis are the mystics of Islam. A long line of Sufi saints in India, Persia, Turkey and other countries have nourished the souls of people through their poetry and songs, which emerge out of their passionate devotion to the Supreme. The presence of the Sacred, the Divine, the Holy, the Eternal is here and everywhere; is now and for ever. The Sufis are in love with the Supreme. They seek and find the Beloved in every moment of their lives. They drink the wine of love. They are intoxicated with love. They live in ecstasy. For them the Supreme appears in the blossoming flower, the flowing river, falling leaves and shining stars; these are the faces of the Beloved. No wonder the Maulana has no problem with Hindus. No wonder that he cannot understand why Muslims should be antagonistic to anybody.

Sufism has always been a unifying force. The Sufi saints have been and continue to be shared and revered by Hindus and Muslims alike, across India and Pakistan. Therefore, seeing Hindus and Muslims fighting makes the Maulana's soul cry in deep pain. The great Sufi master and poet Rumi, born in Afghanistan and brought up in Turkey, is the hero of Maulana Wahiduddin. It was Rumi who wrote:

The Sufi opens his hands to the universe
and gives away each instant, free.
Unlike someone who begs on the street for money to survive,
a dervish begs to give you his life.[13]

And so Wahiduddin wishes to pour out his heart and give his life in love, because like Rumi he believes that 'the One I love is everywhere'. Loving God means loving every creature upon the Earth, even the worms and butterflies. Then what of the Hindus? Rumi wrote:

Inside the Great Mystery that is,
we don't really own anything.
What is this competition we feel then,
before we go, one at a time, through the same gate?[14]

As I WALKED away after my meeting with the Maulana, I reflected on the teachings of Mohammed on anger. The Buddha gave the same teachings.

One day a disciple asked for the Buddha's blessings so that he might reach out to people and sow the seeds of peace. The Buddha readily gave his blessings, and then he said, "You will meet strangers who do not agree with you and may not like your pronouncements on peace. If they abuse you and speak unkindly to you, then be not angry. Instead, be grateful that at least they have not assaulted you physically. If they do assault you, then too be not angry. Instead be grateful that they have not wounded you. If they wound you, even then be not angry. Instead be thankful that they have not killed you. And if you meet such unusually harsh people who do proceed to kill you, then still, my beloved disciple, harbour no anger in your heart. If they kill you, they have liberated you from this body. Body is impermanent and transitory. Cling not to the idea of 'I' and the idea of 'self'. If you are so free in spirit, so liberated from anger, then I bless you my beloved, go and sow the seeds of peace in the hearts and minds of people you meet, without any hesitation or discrimination."

Anger erodes the mind, corrodes the heart, sickens the soul and agitates the body. Therefore, like Mohammed, the Buddha too renounced anger in all circumstances.

He not only instructed his disciples to be free of anger, he freed himself of anger. This was evident when he encountered Angulimal, the killer.

One day, after having spoken to a group of people about compassion in a grove of mango trees outside the town of Rajgir, the Buddha set off on his walk to the next town of Nalanda. Someone warned him, "On that way lives a man who takes pleasure in cruelty, who likes to wear a garland of human fingers."

"I teach compassion to all, without discrimination," said the Buddha. "In particular, I teach compassion to those who appear to be cruel. Teaching compassion to the compassionate is preaching to the converted."

So the Buddha continued on his way to Nalanda. Soon he saw a man with a sharp dagger in his hand and frowns on his forehead. His lips were shaking in anger. He did wear a garland of human fingers! This was Angulimal.

The Buddha stopped and smiled at Angulimal with disarming calm. Seeing someone unperturbed surprised Angulimal. He was used to people running away from him. He had never encountered a person standing still and smiling at him. For the first time in his life he saw a smiling face.

"Why aren't you running away?" he said. "Don't you know who I am? I am Angulimal, the killer." He said proudly, "I am the lover of human blood. I hate humans but I love their fingers." No one had ever listened to Angulimal before. This was a moment, when someone actually stood smiling in front of him.

The Buddha said, "I know who you are. Your fame has spread far and wide. People tremble at the sound of your name. I know you wish to kill me. But thank you for giving me a chance to speak with you. I simply wish to say that when you kill someone, you also harm yourself. Every time you take someone's life you are diminished. You can stop killing, you can be free of anger. Do not fry yourself in the frying pan of anger, Angulimal. Come with me and swim in the sea of compassion. You are capable of compassion and friendship. I want you to realise it, that's all. Now if you wish to kill me, that is your prerogative." Once again the Buddha gave a big smile.

"Do you mean to say that I can live without killing? That there is an alternative?"

This was the beginning of a long and transforming conversation, which ended in Angulimal discarding his dagger and becoming a follower of the Buddha. Thus the Buddha could overcome not only his own anger but also the anger of someone apparently so wicked and evil.

Of course, Jesus Christ, in company with Mohammed and the Buddha, did the same. He urged his followers, "Love thy enemy" and "Turn the other cheek." He said, "Blessed are the meek, for they shall inherit the Earth." Loving your friends, your family and the nice people you like, is all well and good. There is nothing wrong with that: we all like to love and be loved by our kith and kin and friends. But all great religious teachers have shown from their own lives that it is possible to expand our love to include everyone, even those who torment us. Jesus on the cross prayed for the soldiers who were ridiculing and torturing him, "Father forgive them, they know not what they do."

In our own time, the only words Mahatma Gandhi uttered as he was assassinated were "Hey Ram" which means "Glory to God".

This is why Maulana Wahiduddin says, "To be a good Muslim we need to love not just our fellow Muslims but also Hindus, Christians, Jews and the rest. It may be a tall order, but without such vision religion has no meaning whatsoever."

*   *   *

Chapter 19

A Land of Contrasts

*"What seems the strongest has outlived its term. The future lies
with what's affirmed from under."*—Seamus Heaney

IN THE YEAR 2000 I was once again in my native land. My wife June and
daughter Maya were with me and I was filled with excitement and
anticipation.

India is passing through the best of times and the worst of times—
through rising confidence, through declining confidence; through renewal of
its spirit, through loss of its spirit; through clarity of purpose, through confusion of purpose; through a sense of stability and through a sense of turmoil.

The best of India is not in New Delhi; it is a city like any other city—
full of traffic, fumes, speed, shopping, alienation. Behind the walls of cor-
porate headquarters and government offices, still housed in grand buildings, live the elite. They are the bureaucrats, the globalisers and those who
want to turn all of India into places like New Delhi, where people compete
against each other for privilege, wealth and status.

But relative to other Indian cities, New Delhi is spacious and compar-
atively green, and occasionally we could see a cow or two roaming freely
in the midst of crowded streets. There were small craft workshops, small
industries, small businesses and small communities surviving in the sub-
urbs. But the rich and powerful don't seem to like them. The city authorities were busy displacing small-scale and traditional industries. This was
being done in the name of reducing pollution. The government and leaders
of big business refuse to acknowledge that most of the pollution is caused
by their lorries, their cars and their air conditioners. Behind the mask of
improving the environment the government is dispossessing the small and
the weak.

After fifty years of independence the Indian government is still run
under a colonial constitution. The civil service, the police, the education
system and the legal system are, to a large extent, as they were during

British rule. Where are Indian values in governance? What happened to the aspirations and dreams of people like Mahatma Gandhi, who struggled for the empowerment of the masses and not of the few?

There is no shortage of food in India. Millions of tonnes of grain sit in government stores. There is no shortage of talented people—thousands of them are running computer industries and medical services in Europe and America. Therefore, there can be no excuse for men, women, children, young and old, blind and sick, living in slums or on the roadside, to be left to beg in the streets, or to go to bed hungry. But much of Delhi is driven not by the ideals of mutuality, service and caring, but by greed, pride and personal ambition.

Yet there is another side to Delhi. Our friend Rukmini Sekhar invited us to have tea at the Craft Museum. The moment we entered the bamboo gates, it was a different world.

Situated on the Exhibition Grounds of Mathura Road, this rural oasis shows what India could be. Here is a place where human needs are satisfied through the honest labour of weavers, potters, painters, blacksmiths and builders. The glamour of New Delhi soon faded from our minds when we saw the elegant simplicity of craftsmen and women who have been marginalised by an arrogant urban civilisation.

Unfortunately, to benefit from the consumers and tourists of the metropolis, the craftspeople have to leave their homes and camp by their stalls for months. This undermines the integrity of the crafts. It is not how my mother would have envisaged crafts being practised, nor is it how rural India really maintains its craft tradition. Nevertheless, by financing this museum the government is helping to keep these skills alive; and rootless urbanites can at least see creativity, spirituality, beauty and the innocence of craftspeople, a stark contrast to the competitive capitalist system.

We understood the meaning of John Keats' phrase, "Beauty is Truth and Truth Beauty", when we saw artisans practising their crafts which offend no one, harm no one and give pleasure to those who see them and joy to those who use them.

Craftspeople take so little from nature: they waste nothing, they exploit nobody, they create no ugliness and they pollute nowhere. Craft is the culture of non-violence and the true economy of peace. Crafts are the embodiment of ecology and of sustainability. They are the barrier against consumerism. India is fortunate that there are millions of craftspeople still producing objects of the highest quality and making a living. The Indian craft tradition is a most appropriate form of livelihood for the future. If under the influence of machine civilisation, this craft tradition is lost, then India will be lost forever.

GANDHI'S DREAM WAS to base the Indian economy once again on the craft tradition and re-create local economies (*swadeshi*). People outside India know of Gandhi as a champion of India's independence movement, and of his non-violent struggle to end British colonialism. But that was only a small part of his vision. For him there was no point in getting rid of the British while maintaining the British system. He argued that there wouldn't be much difference if the ordinary people of India were to be oppressed by Indian rulers rather than by the British. There would be no point in exchanging white *sahibs* with brown *sahibs*. Real independence for India would only be achieved if there were to be an economy which did not exploit the weak nor destroy natural 'capital'.

The spirit and the soul of India has always rested in her village communities. Gandhi said, "The true India is to be found not in its few cities but in its 700,000 villages. If the villages perish, India will perish too." His vision was of a confederation of self-governing, self-reliant, self-organising and self-employed people living in village communities and smaller towns, deriving their right livelihood from the products of their homesteads and crafts. The maximum economic and political power—including the power to decide what could be imported into or exported from the village community—would remain in the hands of the local Village Councils.

In India people have lived for thousands of years in relative harmony with their surroundings: living in their homesteads, weaving homespun clothes, eating home-grown food and using home-made goods. They cared for their animals, forests and lands. They celebrated the fertility of the soil with feasts, performed the stories of great epics and built magnificent temples. Every region of India has developed its own distinctive culture to which travelling storytellers, wandering sadhus and a constantly flowing stream of pilgrims made their contribution.

Mahatma Gandhi worked to revive this India of local economies. He believed that whatever is made or produced in a village must be used first and foremost by the members of that village. Trading should only be in what is surplus and in exchange for things that cannot be produced in that village. Such trading of goods between villages, towns, regions or nations should be minimal, like icing on a cake. Goods and services which cannot be generated within local communities may be imported from elsewhere, as an exception rather than the rule.

A local economy avoids economic dependence on external market forces which could make the village community vulnerable. It avoids unnecessary, unhealthy, wasteful and environmentally destructive transportation. Gandhi believed that each village should build a strong economic base to satisfy most of its needs, and all members of the community should give priority to their own local goods and services.

When an economy is built on local resources, natural and human, then every community will have its own carpenters, shoemakers, potters, builders, mechanics, engineers, farmers, weavers, teachers, bankers, merchants, musicians and artists. In other words each village would be a microcosm of society as a whole. For Gandhi such local communities and villages were so important that he thought they should be given the status of Village Republics. And yet they should embody the spirit of the home; they should be like an extended family rather than a collection of competing individuals.

The British system in India was to foster centralised, industrialised and mechanised modes of production. Gandhi turned this principle on its head. He envisioned a decentralised, home-grown, local and hand-crafted mode of production. In other words, not mass production but production by the masses.

Local economies (swadeshi) restore the dignity of work. There is an intrinsic value in work by hand. When we are engaged in such work we can give expression to the aesthetic, spiritual and creative aspects of our being. In surrendering to machines in factories we lose an opportunity for creativity and self-fulfilment.

Gandhi wrote, "It is a tragedy of the first magnitude that millions of people have ceased to use their hands as hands. Nature has bestowed on us this great gift, which is our hands. If the craze for machinery methods continues, it is highly likely that a time will come when we shall be so incapacitated and weak that we shall begin to curse ourselves for having forgotten the use of living machines given to us by God. Millions cannot keep fit by games and athletics; and why should they exchange the useful, productive, hardy occupations for the useless, unproductive and expensive sports and games? Mass production is only concerned with the product, whereas production by the masses is concerned with the product, the producer and the process."

Locally based economies in India enhance community spirit, community relationships and community well-being. Such economies encourage mutual aid. Members of the village community take care of themselves, their families, their neighbours, their animals, lands and forests, and all the other natural resources for the benefit of present and future generations.

Mass production has led people to leave their villages, their land, their crafts and homesteads, and migrate to the cities where they end up working in factories. When they stand at the conveyor belts, they become cogs in the machine. It is the system of mass production which has given birth to slums and shanty towns. Fewer and fewer people are needed to work, because the industrial system requires greater productivity with the minimum number of workers.

The money economy is based on efficient machines working faster and faster; as a result many men and women are thrown on the scrap heap of unemployment. Such a society generates rootless and jobless millions, living as dependants on the state or begging in the streets. In a local economy (swadeshi) the machine must be subordinated to the worker; the machine should not become the master, dictating the pace of human activity. Similarly, the market should serve the community rather than forcing people to fit the market.

Globalisation is the opposite of local economies. With globalisation, every nation wishes to export more and import less in order to keep the balance of payments in their favour. This is bound to cause a perpetual economic crisis and perpetual unemployment. Discontent is the result. In order to address this human discontent, a promise of perpetual economic growth and increasing consumer comforts is offered. But contentment, satisfaction and a sense of fulfilment remains a mirage.

Gandhi said, "A certain degree of physical comfort is necessary, but above a certain level it becomes a hindrance instead of a help; therefore, the ideal of creating an unlimited number of wants and satisfying them seems to be a delusion and a trap. The satisfaction of one's physical needs must come at a certain point to a dead stop, before it degenerates into physical decadence. Europeans will have to remodel their outlook if they are not to perish under the weight of the comforts to which they are becoming slaves."

In order to protect economic growth, sources of raw materials and markets for their products, countries go to war. The roots of military conflicts are in economic conflicts. Therefore, if we wish to create a peaceful world, we need to create a peace economy. Gandhi said, "People have to live in village communities and simple homes, rather than desiring to live in palaces." Millions of people will never be able to live at peace with each other if they are constantly fighting for higher and higher standards of living. We cannot have real peace in the world if we look at each other's countries as sources of raw materials or as markets for finished industrial goods. The seeds of war are sown with economic expansion, because the economists and industrialists fail to see when enough is enough. Even when countries reach a very high standard of living, they still pursue the idea of economic growth. Those who do not know when enough is enough will never have enough, no matter how much they have. But, on the other hand, those who know when enough is enough can realise that they already have enough.

A local economy is a peace economy. First of all peace with oneself. With peace of mind, one is free from the constant striving for more and more. Secondly, it fosters peace between peoples, so there is no more frantic competition and take-overs, no more desire to control and dominate. Thirdly, it encourages peace with nature: no more large-scale destruction of forests, pollution of the air and contamination of water. Thus local economies are a peace imperative.

The global economy is just the opposite, as it drives people towards high performance, high achievement and high ambition. This results in stress, loss of meaning, loss of inner peace, loss of time for personal and family relationships and loss of spirituality.

The Indian economy was once embedded in the paradigm of local economies. Agriculture, horticulture, pottery, furniture-making, metalwork, jewellery, leatherwork and many other economic activities were always local. Most prominently, the craft of textiles was at the centre of village life. Each village had its own spinners, carders, dyers and weavers who were at the heart of the local economy. However, when India was flooded with machine-made, mass produced English textiles the indigenous textile production was rapidly put out of business. That is why Gandhi thought it essential that the craft of local and handmade cloth be restored. He chose the spinning-wheel as the symbol of both individual self-reliance and national independence.

Many people argued that it was naïve to think that India's independence could be gained through spinning, because their idea of independence was limited to the change of power from British to Indian hands. But this was never Gandhi's idea. For him, mere change of power, without a change in the economic and political system, was no change at all. He wanted to make people independent of exploitation by the strong and powerful.

Gandhi's spinning-wheel took off. Hundreds of thousands of people from all backgrounds made a bonfire of the mill-made cloth imported from England or made in Indian factories. They learned to spin their own yarn and weave their own cloth. Weaving and the wearing of homespun cloth became a mark of distinction for all those who worked for Indian liberation.

The Craft Museum of New Delhi is a timely reminder of what is at stake and what we are about to lose, if we do not cherish the local craft economy.

FROM NEW DELHI we went to Alwar in Rajasthan, where we were met by Rajendra Singh, a radical Gandhian worker. He drove us through the Sariska Tiger Reserve, and showed us examples of water harvesting which have restored the vitality of the forest and the neighbouring farms. This revival of the forest has increased the wildlife, including the numbers of blue cow, cheetahs, spotted deer, sambar, wild peacocks, wild boar, monkeys and, above all, tigers. The newly created abundance of water has enabled people and tigers to coexist in a wild environment.

Because of the large number of small-scale dams, skilfully built by local people using local materials, this area has regained its supply of water. Water harvesting is India's single most important need, but the government and its agencies have ignored small-scale traditional methods of conserving water in favour of large-scale dams which mainly benefit the cities at the expense of the countryside.

Government engineers and planners love big schemes—big machines and big dams—because they involve big money. But, as is evident in all large-scale dam projects such as the Narmada dams in western India, large numbers of local people have to be displaced, trees in their thousands drowned, tribal cultures decimated and whole landscapes deformed; whereas small-scale dams such as those here in Sariska are low-cost, enhance the landscape and bring back people from the cities to rural areas.

At the beginning of the project, Rajendra Singh and his group had great difficulty in persuading the authorities to allow small-scale and sustainable dams, but with courage they fought the vested interests and won. This is a tale of Two Dams, and shows how the small dams of Sariska are life enhancing and the big dams of Narmada are destructive of land and people.

Rajendra Singh is a gentle hero. He has decided not to marry, not to go for a conventional job, not to seek personal success and not to pursue fame and fortune. Instead he has devoted his life to the service of the ordinary people of Sariska. He knows the hills, the valleys, the trees, the animals and the people of this region intimately. And he loves them. Rajendra represents the best of India. He and his group are an example of the way the work of Gandhi and Vinoba lives on. As long as young people like Rajendra are engaged in the selfless service to the land and its people, there is hope for India.

THEN WE CAME to Jaipur, the famous pink city and the capital of Rajasthan, to meet my mentor and friend, Siddharaj Dhadda, with whom I had worked in the late fifties. At the age of ninety-two he was as active as ever. On the eve of our arrival his wife, Uma, had passed away, aged eighty. Siddharaj was supported and sustained by a large number of friends who came and sat with him from early morning to late evening so that he and his family should not drown in the sorrow of their loss. We joined them and lit incense in front of Uma's photo, which was garlanded with a ring of white, hand-spun cotton.

Downstairs sat Siddharaj with male visitors, upstairs sat the women with the female members of the family. The central courtyard of the spacious house (*havelli*) was filled with the presence of a great neem tree, which provided a sacred setting for the ritual of remembrance.

Seeing Siddharaj was inspiring. He lives with four generations in a joint family household. He spins cotton daily on his spinning-wheel, enough to meet his clothing needs. He has done this ever since he joined Gandhi in the liberation struggle.

After Independence, Siddharaj was a minister in the government of Rajasthan. This he soon renounced in order to join Vinoba's land gift movement, and Siddharaj continues to fight for people's power at the local level. His lifestyle is a true example of simplicity, frugality and elegance.

One of Siddharaj's granddaughters is married into a family of digambara Jains. The monks of this order wear no clothes at all. This is the ultimate mark of renunciation of all possessions. With the family we went to see their guru, who was surrounded by lay men and women.

We asked the guru, "What is the meaning of living without any possessions, not even a loincloth?"

He replied, "This is a symbol of non-violence, of non-defence, of no protection against anything, of utter vulnerability. It is a way of overcoming fear, shame and vanity. However, even though renunciation of clothes is difficult, it is nothing if the monk has not renounced the inner baggage of ego, pride and self-righteousness. Renunciation of external things is only a way to lead us into renunciation of internal attachments."

The digambara way of life is an experiment in extreme austerity. The sky-clad monks not only do not wear clothes, they do not use a mat, mattress or blanket for sleeping, even in winter. They sleep on a bare wooden bench. They may not sleep on their back or their front, in order to avoid exposure or stimulation of the sexual organs. They do not change position from one side to the other in case their body should cause harm to the minutest creature. A bent arm under the head is the only pillow they have. Once they are awake they get up; they do not remain lying down to fall asleep again.

They take food once a day in their cupped hands, given by lay disciples. Every six months they pluck out the hair from their heads and beards with their own hands as a practice to overcome the fear of pain. They walk barefoot in heat and cold. They are a supreme example of reducing one's physical needs to the bare minimum. There are only about fifty such sky-clad monks in the whole of India.

Siddharaj said to us, "One can easily be sceptical about the relevance of such practices to the modern world. But where has the limitless accumulation, possession and consumption of material objects taken us? The extreme example of the digambara monks can inspire others to follow a less consumerist path."

Chapter 20

Temples of Delight

RAJASTHAN IS A LAND of Jains, who avoid killing even an ant. Rajasthan is also a land of Rajputs—a caste of warriors who fight to the finish to defend their honour. The idea of non-violence is no part of their armoury.

Jains and Rajputs have cultivated these parallel cultures in the same soil: one passive, the other active. The dynamic and heroic quality of the Rajput warriors is attractive. Their sense of dignity and selflessness is exemplary. Mahavir too was a Rajput. But for Mahavir the real battlefield is not outside of us: it is within. Conquering one's own inner desire to control others is the real victory. The true act of heroism is to overcome ego, vanity and anger. So Mahavir did not renounce warriorship—he changed the rules of engagement. He 'fought' against the forces of ignorance and he did so with the 'weapon' of non-violence.

Jains share many of the Rajput qualities. There is much common ground upon which the two traditions have been built: for example, self-sacrifice in the service of others, and helping others in their time of need. The important difference is that Jains renounce the use of violence: there is no compromise. For them, the ends cannot justify the means. Under no circumstances can a Jain take up arms and kill, whereas the Rajputs will fight for justice, for honour, and for what is right.

But times have changed; modern methods of fighting are so impersonal and mechanical that the ideal of a heroic soldier is hardly relevant. In modern warfare bombs are dropped from thousands of feet, indiscriminately killing soldiers, civilians and animals and destroying the natural world. Therefore the challenge now for Rajputs is to marry their dynamism with non-violence and to use it as a soul force. Similarly, the Jains need to emerge from their passivity so that non-violence can become a dynamic and effective force for change. As Mahatma Gandhi showed, non-violence is not cowardice: courage and inner strength are the hallmarks of non-violence.

WE TRAVELLED to Rajsamund, a lakeside town a few hundred miles south-west of Jaipur. Along the national highway we passed hundreds of marble mines blighting the landscape, with white dust everywhere covering the leaves of trees. This dust not only renders the soil unusable for farming, but chokes the woods and the land. Diggers are taking away whole hillsides, a very violent way to treat the environment. To make way for mining, trees have been felled, the water table has dropped, and the great lake of Rajsamund, which has never dried since it was created in 1660, has dwindled to a tiny pond.

Admittedly, some local people have benefited in terms of wages and jobs, but at what cost to their land, their health, their culture and their communities? Middlemen come from all over India to acquire mining rights and make profits. So, the real beneficiaries are the rich in the cities like Delhi and Mumbai, who build palatial homes with cheap marble—at the cost of the people of Rajsamund.

Near Rajsamund we visited the famous temple of Lord Vishnu, Preserver of the World, in the town of Nathadwara. Our host S. L. Gandhi said, "People worship the blue image of Vishnu at this temple because blue is the colour of infinite beauty. Blue Vishnu is as vast as the blue sky and as deep as the blue ocean. Whenever the world is in trouble, the power of Vishnu is activated to restore the balance. Radha and Krishna are incarnations of Vishnu. He is always present because he is the personification of the sun, the god of light; he is husband of Lakshmi, the goddess of abundance; he is father of Kama, the god of love. Vishnu rides on the sacred bird Garuda, the eagle, and sleeps on the bed of Sesha, the serpent. People adore Vishnu because he is the embodiment of life, love and beauty. *Darshan* of Vishnu at this temple will bring you joy and delight."

As we walked through the temple precincts, S. L. Gandhi continued, "The eighteenth-century image of Vishnu was brought to the town of Nathadwara in order to protect it from the assault of the Moghul Emperor Aurangzeb. At that time Delhi and Agra were already in the hands of Moghul kings, and the town of Mathura between the two cities was in danger of attack. So overnight the devotees of the Lord Vishnu carried away the sacred image, looking for a safe haven. The kingdom of Jaipur was already in alliance with the Moghuls. The only Rajput king resisting the Moghul influence was Rana Pratap, the king of this region. So the image was kept in a small town under his rule."

Although our friend S. L. Gandhi is a devout Jain, this was no barrier to his being enthusiastic about this Hindu temple. He went on with the legend, "After many years, when an attempt was made to move the image of Vishnu to a bigger and better temple, the vehicle sank in the gateway, indicating that the Lord Vishnu preferred to stay where he was. So the place became known as the temple to the Lord of the Gate. Because of this incident, the reputation of the temple reached far and wide and, ever since that time, pilgrims have been pouring in to get a glimpse of the god when the gates are briefly and sporadically opened."

We were extremely lucky to catch a glimpse (darshan) of the sacred image. The dark blue statue of Vishnu was adorned with well crafted ornaments. Flowers, fruit, lamps and incense in the temple created a sensual experience of colour, smell and sound, while the devotion of eager pilgrims produced a mystical atmosphere.

Rice artists, outside the temple, engrave the name of the Lord on grains of rice. Pilgrims take home the sacred grains that are believed to encapsulate the living qualities of Lord Vishnu. These grains of rice are the microcosm of the macrocosm: the world on a grain of rice.

FROM RAJSAMUND WE DROVE to Mount Abu, which was the favourite hill station of the Rajput kings and queens. It is also a sacred site for Jains and Hindus.

Legend has it that Nakki Lake, situated on the summit of Mount Abu, was dug by the gods using no other tools than their nails. For them, speed was no object; in fact, the slower the digging, the better the ritual of creating a pond for the holy water where angels, humans, animals and birds could quench their thirst, clean their bodies and purify their souls.

The Jain temples, however, were built by humans and elephants. Dozens of elephants made numerous journeys to carry white marble up the mountain. To thank the elephants for their contribution, a pavilion to them was erected just opposite the main entrance. It is known as the Abode of the Elephants. The builders, the carvers, the patrons and the mahouts are all figured here in marble, in acknowledgement of their work.

Known as Dilwara, there are five temples in the complex. The first and most exquisite was built in the eleventh century and is dedicated to Adinath, the first of the twenty-four great spiritual guides (tirthankaras). There are forty-eight elegant carved pillars—twenty-four devoted to the tirthankaras and twenty-four dedicated to their associated animals—which symbolise the inseparable connection between the human world and the world of other beings. This eternal and unchangeable relationship of interdependence between all beings—humans, animals and divine—is at the heart of Jain temple worship.

The second temple is dedicated to tirthankara Neminath, another great spiritual guide. This temple is an architectural jewel. The ceilings support fantastic carvings of myths and stories, gods and goddesses, flowers and trees, animals and birds. One of the carvings is of a lotus flower hanging from the centre of the dome. It is difficult to imagine that this flower was carved from solid rock; it is an incredible piece of work. The craftsmanship of polishing the stone is such that even after hundreds of years it still glows.

The underlying message of the artisans is that working with diligence and patience brings out the qualities of devotion. While carving the stone, one works on oneself to illuminate the purity of the soul. The realisation of art is an outer manifestation of self-realisation. For Jains there is no such thing as 'art for art's sake'. All art, for them, is art for devotion, for contemplation, for meditation, for celebration and for manifestation of the spirit. Jain art, not only the images and sculptures in temples but also the miniatures and illustrations in sacred scriptures, has tremendous sensuality. It is a paradox that these champions of asceticism should produce works of such exuberant and intricate vividness.

In the middle ages in Europe, people created art for God's sake. When religion began to wane, art was created for the sake of human glorification. In the twentieth century people talked of art for art's sake. And in post-modern times the trend is art for the artist's sake, where the personality of the artist has become paramount, and the glory of the divine is nowhere to be seen. Even skill, craftsmanship and beauty have been squeezed out of 'art'.

From the outside it is impossible to imagine that these temples are there, hidden within the rough rock. As you come close, the external appearance is inconspicuous and discreet. This outer simplicity of the architecture indicates that it is the inner quality that matters, not the outer appearance.

WE HURRIED FROM the temples to see the sunset with our host Nagaraja. We stood at 4,000 feet overlooking the vast plains of Rajasthan, etched with fields and lakes, and the fiery ball of the sun created multiple colours at the horizon.

"One wonders", said Nagaraja, "why people in India are chasing oil, gas, electricity and wood, when we could be gathering the energy of the sun. If we could return to worshipping Lord Vishnu in the form of the sun many of our energy problems would be solved. But this is too simple a solution. Modern civilisation loves to complicate things. It seeks what is scarce and ignores what is abundant. Harvesting the sunlight and rainwater makes common sense. But common sense is no longer common. Or is it that our educated elite cannot bring themselves down to the level of commoners? Living by the sun, and developing a reverential relationship with it, may be more important than building highways, mining marble and exploding the atom bomb."

We stayed in the guest house of the Brahma Kumaris, literally 'The

Divine Daughters'. This is a religious group led by women who practise and preach spiritual renewal and social improvement all over the world.

They, to our happy surprise, do use the sun to heat water and cook for thousands of their devotees. They have the world's largest solar cooker in operation. We went to the kitchen at Abu Road, where hundreds of volunteers were preparing lunch by means of gas generated by solar reflectors. If the Brahma Kumaris can feed 5,000 devotees with food cooked with energy from the sun, surely the rest of India should be able to follow suit? Why are Indian industrialists and the government spending precious foreign exchange to import oil? Not because the country is lacking in natural resources, but because the people in power suffer from a failure of the imagination.

The Brahma Kumaris use their imagination not only to feed their members and visitors physically but also to feed them spiritually. Theirs is a movement of spiritual renewal through meditation and through overcoming the forces of ego, anger and greed.

The founder of this group, Brahma Baba, was a diamond merchant in Sind. One day he had a revelation. He simply saw that no amount of diamonds could bring him inner satisfaction or peace of mind. He realised that the way to human happiness is to see the sacred in everyday life and find fulfilment through service to others. He called it *raja yoga*, and established a spiritual university at Mount Abu in the middle of the last century. Now there are 4,000 centres in India and around the world, where tens of thousands of people are practising meditation and a communal lifestyle based on raja yoga.

Nagaraja explained to us, "Yoga is the fundamental principle of the universe and the foundation of Indian philosophy, and we follow it to the best of our ability. Yoga simply means 'uniting'; it means connecting, bringing together and relating. The joining of things or numbers together is yoga. There are two key methods for making our lives wholesome, yoga and viyoga. Yoga means synthesis and viyoga means analysis. We begin with synthesis and afterwards, if necessary, use the method of analysis. That is the correct order."

"How many yogas are there?" I asked.

"There are many kinds of yoga, but six of them are widely known. The first is yoga of the body (*hatha yoga*). In this you hold your feet with your hands, you put your head on your knees, and so on. This way all parts of the body connect with each other, and through that connection you are able to relax and gain health."

"Do you practise this body yoga?" I asked.

"Yes, and one of my favourites is the lotus position. In this posture you put your right foot on your left thigh and your left foot on the right thigh, and put your right palm on your left palm, in your lap. Shoulders relaxed, neck free and spine straight. This is a perfect posture for meditation. When you put right foot on left thigh and left on right, you hardly know which one is right and which one is left. They are in perfect relationship. They are united. Thus the body enters the yoga of the relationship of opposites.

"When people in India meet they greet each other by putting their two palms together and bowing. Again, this is a way of bringing left and right together, I and you together, human and divine together. In this relationship we are in harmony with each other."

"And the next one?" I asked impatiently.

"The second is the yoga of action (*karma yoga*). When we are able to act with our body, mind and spirit in harmony, we become Karma yogis.

"The third is the yoga of meditation (*dhyana yoga*). Action and meditation belong together, like sound and silence. There is no opposition between action and meditation. As we walk on two legs, we live in two states: movement and stillness.

"The fourth is the yoga of knowledge (*gyana yoga*). The word knowledge is too narrow. Gyana is much broader; it includes wisdom, understanding, intuition and insight.

"The fifth is the yoga of devotion (*bhakti yoga*). The yoga of devotion by itself can lead to dogmatism and fundamentalism. Knowledge alone can lead to cynicism and scepticism. Therefore the yoga of knowledge and the yoga of devotion should complement each other.

"The last of the six is *raja yoga*; it means the king of yogas. In raja yoga all five yogas come together.

"Sometimes people emphasise one form of yoga. That is fine as a matter of practicality. But in our deep consciousness we need to realise that by separating one yoga from another we are defeating the very meaning of yoga, which is the joining of things. In the great picture of yoga, all aspects of life are included; there is nothing outside of yoga."

*   *   *

Chapter 21

A Culture of Crafts

*"The artist is not a special kind of person, but every person is
a special kind of artist."*—A. Coomaraswamy

FROM MOUNT ABU we came to Ahmedabad, the capital of Gujarat. The city
was once the textile capital of India, but now that industry has largely disappeared. What is left is the wonderful collection of textiles at the Calico
Museum.

Antique and modern textiles, rare tapestries, wall hangings, woven
tents and canopies, embroidered coverings for elephants, embroidered coverings for chariots for pulling the images of the gods and goddesses were
all there. Saris of every conceivable weave, warp, weft and colour. We were
particularly struck by a thin white cloth, which seemed like a plain cloth
until the guide lit a light behind it. Suddenly an amazing appliqué pattern
was revealed: trees, birds, animals, humans, all made of white thread,
emerging like a whole universe out of a piece of white cloth, like Blake's
poem:

> "To see a world in a grain of sand
> And a heaven in a wild flower
> Hold infinity in the palm of your hand
> And eternity in an hour."

WE STAYED AT the guest house of Gujarat Vidya Peeth, a university established by Mahatma Gandhi in the 1930s. By that time much of India's
formal education was anglicised, but Gandhi thought that the English
education system could not serve an independent India.

With the introduction of British education, the learning of the 'three
Rs'—reading, writing and arithmetic, became the guiding principle. As a
result of this the Indian system of apprenticeship, family crafts, the learning of Sanskrit, religion and philosophy were undermined. Lord Macaulay,

introducing the India Education Act in the British Parliament said, "A single shelf of a good European library is worth the whole native literature of India. . . . Neither as a language of the law nor as a language of religion, has the Sanskrit any particular claim to our engagement. . . . We must do our best to form a class of persons, Indian in blood and colour but English in taste, in opinions, in morals and in intellect."

When this kind of education was imposed by the British Raj, local schools were replaced by colonial schools. At the universities, learning in the English language dominated. Wealthy Indians were sent to public schools and universities in England. And even those who studied in India learned English poetry, English law and English customs, to the neglect of their own Indian culture and crafts. Reading Shakespeare became more important than reading the Indian classics.

Mahatma Gandhi's vision was to create a balanced system where learning by doing would be as essential as learning by reading; education of the hands would be as important as education of the head. Development of the heart would be valued as much as the development of the mind.

According to the Mahatma, British education begins with analysis, whereas Indian education begins with synthesis. The purpose of British education was to oil the wheels of bureaucracy and commerce, which emphasised individualism and personal success. The Indian system was founded to seek spiritual meaning and to develop a sense of community. British education created a hierarchy of professions. At the higher level were office workers, bureaucrats and bankers, who were better paid. At the lower level were farmers, weavers, potters and barbers, who were valued less and paid less.

In Gandhi's view this was erroneous. The skills of intellectuals and manual workers must be valued equally. There should be no division between manual workers and mental workers. Furthermore, the latter need to learn to participate in manual work and vice versa. Thus Gujarat Vidya Peeth was established to train young Indian men and women in manual as well as mental skills, in social skills as well as spiritual ones. For Gandhi, knowledge was a way to learn humility and truth. Gandhi discarded the idea that "knowledge is power"; he believed that knowledge should be an instrument of service. The knowledge that brings arrogance is not true knowledge.

Gujarat Vidya Peeth was the first university where learning took place in the local native languages, Gujarati and Hindi. Alongside their academic training, teachers and students participated in cleaning, cooking, spinning and community service.

Alas, this is now history. In spite of India's independence, a system of Gandhian education never came into being. It is the tragedy of India: the flag changed, but the system remained the same. The Indian government

left the British system of education intact. It took over the educational initiatives started by national leaders, such as that by Gandhi at Gujarat
Vidya Peeth, and corrupted them. The bureaucracy lured them with grants
of money in order to prevent education based on the Indian tradition.
Exams and curricula which gave high status to intellectual pursuits, and no
status to manual work, were imposed.

Yet some of Gandhi's ideals still linger. We saw teachers sitting on cushions on the floor with students engaged in intimate conversations. This was
the class in Jainism, which reminded us of traditional scenes where student
participation, oral communication and deep questioning formed an essential ingredient for learning.

Hospitality, a friendly atmosphere and courtyards with tall, mature
trees made us feel that the spirit of Gandhi was still present here.

GANDHI'S ASHRAM ON the bank of the Sabarmathi river is just down the
road. It is visited by large numbers of people every day. The ashram was
founded in 1918 when Gandhi came back from South Africa, and it was
from this ashram that the long struggle for India's independence began.
When Gandhi left the ashram on his famous salt march he declared that he
would never return to this ashram, his home, until India was free from
British rule. However, many of his friends and colleagues continued to live
there, and today there is still a community engaged in handicrafts, gardening, education and, particularly, the spinning and weaving of handmade
cloth (*khadi*).

At the time of Gandhi, Ahmedabad was India's most famous textile
town, where cotton mills were taking away the livelihoods of spinners and
weavers. Like William Blake and William Morris, Gandhi was against
those 'satanic mills', and initiated a strong campaign to renew India's craft
traditions. Tens of thousands of people gathered to hear Gandhi speak in
the dry river-bed by the ashram. The photos of these meetings and of
Gandhi's life and the campaign for freedom fill the rooms of the museum.
The spinning-wheel became the emblem of the independence movement
and was put on the flag of the National Congress Party. Spinning was a
metaphor for all village crafts, and now, in spite of the fact that the Indian
government treats handicraft as a poor relation of industrial manufacture,
craftspeople of India are rising to claim their rightful place in Indian life.

IT GAVE US great pleasure to visit a craft market in the city, where artisans
were selling jewellery from Jaipur, pottery from the Punjab, bangles from
Bihar, paintings from Bengal, shawls from Gujarat, blankets from
Jaisalmer and hundreds of other items from all over India. These crafts

combined beauty with utility and durability. There was integrity between art and craft, form and function, ethics and aesthetics. When work is done well, done with love and care, done with skill and spirit, then work is transformed into art.

At this craft market we met a young artist from Bengal, Bali Chitrakar, who was showing and selling his own work as well as that of his parents. Their paintings illustrate stories from the Ramayana and the Mahabharata. Bali sang the stories as he unfolded long vertical scrolls depicting sequences of events. One scroll was devoted to the life of Rama, his exile in the forest, his wife Sita being tempted by a golden deer, the eagle trying to prevent Ravana from stealing Sita, the war between Rama and Ravana, and so on. The whole Ramayana was illustrated on one scroll in a sequence of forty pictures. As the young artist sang in deep devotion to Rama, his face took on the expression of ecstasy and we were moved to tears.

There was another stall, run by artists from the district of Madhubani in Bihar. By the time we bought two pictures from them, they had invited us to their homes and asked us to help them to restore respect for village artists. They said: "Our art is either ignored or turned into a commodity, and then a few artists are isolated from the rest and promoted while other artists are ignored and undermined. This is not our way. For us art is not a business, it is a way of life. Together with farming, weaving and home-building we also engage in singing, painting and storytelling. This is a continuum of life. Art is not a separate activity."

HAVING BEEN INSPIRED by the artisans at the craft market, we were fortunate to meet Haku Shah, who works in the tradition of the artist-craftsman. Haku is a short man wearing a hand-spun loose long shirt and thin white trousers. Though in his early sixties, he has a childlike quality of openness and enthusiasm, as well as being a man of decorum. We met him in his studio, which is part of his home and was light and spacious. This medium-sized room doubled as his living room, and occasionally as a sleeping room for guests. He lived there with his wife Vilu.

Haku is a painter, a poet, a curator and a potter. He learned to appreciate the beauty and simplicity of rural life and folk art. He said, "The potential for artistic creativity is present in every man and woman," but unfortunately our utilitarian and industrial civilisation has taken the arts out of everyday life. Painting, drawing, dancing, singing, acting, building and all manner of making have become 'unnecessary' luxuries. In the wake of mass production and mass consumption, the arts have become a hobby rather than a way of life."

For Haku, art is neither a hobby nor a luxury, but an essential ingredient of living and being. In his view, "The work of true artists is to be found not so much in museums and art galleries, but in the rural and tribal communities of India. These people may appear to be 'uncivilised' and illiterate, but in their arts and crafts they have a profound culture."

Haku was born in a village in Gujarat. He was educated at a Gandhian school, where he learnt drawing, spinning, cleaning and many other manual skills. The ideals of Mahatma Gandhi which were taught at the school, such as simplicity, solidarity and service to others, made a lasting impression on him. He went through many struggles. When he was at college he had very little money. Once he did not have enough to buy rice, so instead he bought an inexpensive snack for his lunch, but the moment he opened the packet a bird—a kite—flew over and took it away. Just the wrapper remained in his hand! He had very few clothes at that time, for example only one pair of underpants, so he would wash them in the evening and wear them the next day. With such an upbringing, he understands the plight of poor artists in the villages of India, and respects their integrity.

Haku sees as much beauty and elegance in the pictures on the mud walls of rural dwellings as in the classic carvings of temples. He finds a sense of grace in the decorated clay figures made by artisans in remote, rural areas. As a result he has become a spokesman for the unknown and unrecognised artists of indigenous communities. "It is beauty which has saved India in the past, and it is beauty which will save India in the future," said Haku.

As a painter in the traditional mode, Haku Shah uses exquisite colours to convey a sense of calm contemplation. A tree, a cow and a flute appear and reappear in his paintings as a constant theme. They evoke the ancient mythologies of India. A human figure plays the flute, standing under a tree beside a cow, totally in tune with nature, at ease with himself, and in harmony with the animal kingdom.

"The purpose of art is to connect," says Haku Shah. "We need to connect with our intimate selves, as well as with the entire universe. Music, represented by the flute, is the bridge which connects. Sound is sacred; it feeds the soul and the imagination."

Haku communicates a deep sense of relationship between the human, the natural and the spiritual.

"Art is a combination of love, skill and attention," he says. "Love is the quality of surrender: no holding back, but letting go and allowing something to come through you. Skill comes through regular practice; day after day you have to devote yourself to it. Then art also requires you to pay attention—it is like meditation. Your mind has to be fully present."

Haku Shah sees art as a way of celebrating life, community, nature and the divine.

"What is the source of inspiration for your art?" I asked.

"Nature is always inspiring," said Haku. "In India, people have always considered nature as the true teacher. It is believed that when someone asked the Buddha, 'From whom should we learn compassion and forgiveness?' the Buddha pointed to the Earth and said: 'Earth is compassionate, ever forgiving and always generous.' "

So Haku takes his inspiration from nature for his paintings and poetry. He read us two poems: one was a dialogue between a young girl and an ant, and the other a dialogue between a girl and a bird.

Haku worked at Gujarat Vidya Peeth for many years, and there he collected the arts and crafts of the tribal people of Gujarat. Through that work he won public recognition for vernacular art and craft. As long as there are artists like Haku around, true Indian art will remain in good heart.

It was reassuring to learn that the modern art world also appreciates Haku's work. Haku is one of a very few artists who are able to paint without any concern for fashion, and yet are able to touch contemporary sensibilities.

Fame and recognition have come to Haku even though he has always shied away from them. As Thoreau said, "Success usually comes to those who are too busy to be looking for it." Although his work has been shown in important galleries in Mumbai and Delhi, New York and London, his lifestyle remains unchanged. He has lived in the same simple house for the past thirty years. His living room is his studio, which contains his bare essentials. He is what the *Gita* would describe as a 'Sage of Settled Intelligence'.

*   *   *

Chapter 22

To Be a Pilgrim

FROM AHMEDABAD, early in the morning, we started our bus journey to Palitana, a small town near the south coast of Gujarat. It took us five hours to reach our destination. This is the most sacred place of pilgrimage for Jains. A pilgrimage to Palitana, according to tradition, is considered equal to ten pilgrimages to any other holy site. For liberation from the forces of attachment, and for the realisation of peace and joy within, one needs to come to Palitana and meditate on the holy mountain of Shatrunjaya.

We stayed in one of the many Jain guest houses whose rooms are available free of charge. Their construction was paid for by wealthy Jain families, and they are available to any pilgrim as their gift (*dana*).

At six o'clock the next morning we started our ascent of Mount Shatrunjaya. The 2,000-foot climb is made easy by nearly 3,000 steps. With each step pilgrims contemplate the movement upwards, towards a state of enlightenment where pain and pleasure, sorrow and happiness, loss and gain can no longer disturb. As we climbed, the sun was climbing in the sky. In this luminous dawn, our hearts too were illuminated.

Some of our fellow pilgrims were walking barefoot, as their adherence to non-violence did not allow them to wear shoes made of leather. "Touching the holy ground with the bare skin of your feet connects you to the spirit of the place," explained a pilgrim.

After more than an hour of climbing we reached the top, where the 900 temples were buzzing with thousands of devotees. The most sacred is the temple of Adinath.

As they entered the temple, the pilgrims rang the bell, offered flowers, lit lamps, and joined the chanting of mantras while fingering rosaries. In the precinct, some of them were seated on the ground at little low wooden tables. Using rice grains they formed religious symbols. When they finished their art meditation, they would return the rice grains to the pot placed near the table, ready for the next pilgrim. Even though impermanent, this art is a sacred path of prayer and devotion.

Behind the temple is the sacred tree, believed to be the one under which Adinath sat and obtained enlightenment. Pilgrims continuously circumambulated the tree, in the belief that their souls would be liberated by the power of the sacred tree.

Around this temple there are images of the other twenty-three enlightened masters and spiritual guides (*tirthankaras*). Some of them are standing statues, some seated in meditation. They were carved from white or black marble, or red or yellow stone. This indicates that enlightenment is achieved by all the races of humanity. One of these great teachers was a woman, Mallinath, affirming that gender is no barrier to enlightenment.

Pilgrims believe that the simplest way to obtain self-liberation is the way of devotion (*bhakti*). The surrender of ego, individuality, even of identity, to Adinath, establishes a state in which there is no separation between the pilgrim and the divine. Bhakti motivates the pilgrim to go to Palitana and climb the mountain. Some pilgrims climb to the peak once a day, some go at dawn and dusk, and some repeat the climb as often as they can, in spite of the heat of the sun, taking only a short rest between each climb.

At any one time there are over 1,000 monk and nun pilgrims staying in the town, who practise bhakti. And there is a continuous flow of lay pilgrims who find the peace and purity of this place utterly captivating. Having refreshed themselves in this atmosphere of devotion, they can return to their everyday life re-enchanted and reinvigorated.

Halfway down the mountain we visited the temple of Padmavati. She is the protective deity of the twenty-third enlightened master (tirthankara), Parshwanath. Padmavati is the goddess of grace and protects all pilgrims. Her name means the lotus spirit: as the lotus is tender, multi-petalled and pure, so is goddess Padmavati. Those who invoke her spirit will attain lotus qualities.

The attendant of the temple, giving us blessing, explained, "The lotus is the symbol of detachment. The lotus grows out of the mud, and yet no mud can stick on the lotus. So negativity cannot stick to a pilgrim who is devoted to Padmavati. A state of equanimity within reveals our gentle lotus qualities. It is up to us whether we sit on the soft seat of lotus or on the hard bed of nails. Life is what we make of it. A lotus life is a life of beauty, colour and petals of joy. Padmavati asks the pilgrims, 'I am lotus: are you? If not, why not?'"

We sat facing the image of Goddess Padmavati for some time. We contemplated the lotus, and wondered why we hit our heads against the rocks of ego and then bleed with sorrow, when we are capable of letting go and of being as soft and serene as a lotus.

We said to Padmavati, "Yes, Goddess, yes; why not? Why not be lotus when we are lotus?" With sighs of relief we bowed to Goddess Padmavati.

THE NEXT MORNING we were invited by Jayu Shah to a Jain guest house where pilgrims are offered a meal for one rupee. It is a token charge so that pilgrims don't feel embarrassed to be given something free—but in effect it is a gift so that the act of pilgrimage can be undertaken by rich and poor alike.

Jayu Shah had been a businessman and a diamond trader in Mumbai. One day he decided that he had had enough; money-making was not worth his time. He renounced the pursuit of affluence and decided to live a life of service. Now he walks barefoot, sleeps on the floor on a mat, and takes care of pilgrims.

We joined Jayu for a simple breakfast of local bread, sun-dried vegetables and fresh milk. Jayu ate every bit of food and wiped the metal dish meticulously clean with his fingers, and pouring some water from his glass he rinsed the plate and drank the water. He explained that this is the Jain way of finishing the meal so that nothing is wasted and there will be hardly any washing up to do! He was a perfect example of Jain simplicity.

Afterwards he took us to see his latest project, some ten miles away from Palitana. It is a cow sanctuary (*goshala*). The state of Gujarat was suffering from drought: for the past three years there had been no rain. The farmers were unable to afford to keep their cattle, so they brought scores of animals daily to this goshala. Jayu welcomed them. Already over 4,000 cows and bullocks were being fed and housed. Jayu was preparing to take up to 10,000 animals. He had raised money to dig wells and to buy food. 2,000 trees had been planted on the site. The animals were being well looked after by a team of devoted workers. The place was clean; the cow dung was gathered twice a day and turned into fuel or compost. We saw thousands of cattle with enormous horns standing side by side peacefully and in good temper, chewing their cud—with no sign of aggressiveness. They seemed to know that they were in a safe haven.

Jayu explained to us, "Cows are an essential part of our economy: they provide milk, fuel, compost and bullocks for threshing and ploughing. Bullocks are also the workers for pressing oil in the village oil press. Bullocks transport more goods than all the Indian freight trains put together. Therefore, Jains take great care and show their compassion in providing for these cows. What is more, when cows are old and no longer giving milk, we look after them at specially built old cows' homes." Jayu did not seem to discriminate between his devotion to religion, to his guests and to cows. "While taking care of cows, you learn to take care of everything. You become a caring person," said Jayu. "Caring for the cows is good economy, and a good wholesome economy is good religion."

"When the drought is over, what will happen to these cattle?" I asked.

"Then the farmers will come and take their cows back home. Those who are left with us we will take care of, up to the end."

JAYU WAS A follower of a Jain monk called Hitaruchi, who was staying in a town some ten miles away. Jayu arranged a car to take us there. Before he became a monk, Hitaruchi too was a diamond merchant. (Many Jains seem to deal in diamonds!) After many years of trading, he heard an inner calling, "Will you find true meaning in these stones? Why not deal in true diamonds? The diamonds of compassion, love and truth."

Hitaruchi threw his diamonds into the street and took vows of poverty. He became a wandering monk with a begging bowl.

There was a buzz in the room where we met Hitaruchi. A number of young monks were in the room, sitting on soft cream-coloured blankets, studying. Hitaruchi was immediately distinguishable from the rest. He radiated an aura of sainthood, of calm and ease. He was almost emaciated because of his austere lifestyle, yet he was lively, vigorous and gregarious. His eyes were bright and contented. His expressions revealed a sense of assurance and confidence in himself and his way of life.

Around his waist he wore an unbleached unstitched hand-spun cloth, which reached to his ankles. There was a similar piece of cloth around his torso. He held in his hand a small piece of cloth which he would use to cover his mouth when speaking, in order to avoid any harm to minute and microscopic insects in the air.

Hitaruchi had a clothbound book open in front of him, placed on a wooden stand. There was a single-minded commitment, unwavering faith and heartfelt devotion emanating from his eyes. The atmosphere very much reminded me of my young days when I was a monk.

We were invited to sit down in front of him and have a conversation.

"What is the message of Jainism to the world?" I asked

"In one word, non-violence," said muni Hitaruchi. "It is the perennial teaching, nothing new, but we need to reinterpret and revive it again and again. We need to deepen our understanding of it and above all to practise it with diligence.

"Non-violence begins in the mind, in thought, in speech and in every-day life. It is not just a pious doctrine but a way of life, and only through the practice of non-violence can one find true peace. Non-violence is the seed principle as well as the supreme principle. Non-violence is not harming others for their sakes, as well as not harming others for one's own sake. When we harm others we are harming ourselves," said Hitaruchi.

"Non-violence is seen by many Jains as a matter of personal conduct," I observed.

"Yes, but that is not enough. Non-violence is not just a matter of personal behaviour. Non-violence must include the social, political, economic and ecological dimensions. Social injustice, political oppression, wasteful industrial production and destruction of natural resources, are all violence."

"With this message", Hitaruchi continued, "we are walking from village to village asking people to seek contentment in quality of life rather than in the quantity of material possessions.

"Many Jains are Jains in name only; their understanding of Jain principles is paper thin. They have become bounded by rituals without the living practice." As a step towards the practice of non-violence, muni Hitaruchi wears organically grown cotton. He has persuaded farmers to grow cotton without chemicals, and many spinners and weavers to make the cloth by hand and keep it unbleached. This is a true revival of Gandhian homespun cloth (*khadi*).

"Nowadays khadi is being made with inorganic cotton, mixed with polyester and bleached. What a travesty!" Hitaruchi protested.

The monk encourages his followers to undertake pilgrimages on foot with him, in simplicity. No cars, trucks, lorries or jeeps are used to carry their tents, food and other belongings, as "these fossil-fuel-guzzling means of transportation are most violent to the Earth." Only the least violent and traditional means are employed, such as bullock carts. Better still, they carry their bags on their backs!

Hitaruchi and his followers walk every year from Ahmedabad to Palitana and back. Over 1,000 people walk with him. Along the way they eat only organic food, cooked with renewable fuels such as wood or cow-dung fires. No electricity, kerosene, petrol or gas is used. The utensils employed are not made in high-tech factories (no stainless steel, nor plastic), and all pots, pans and plates are made of copper or bronze, the traditional metals commonly used in India. The utensils were all made by hand in small workshops. This was an example of practising purity of means for purity of ends.

* * *

Chapter 23

In the Footsteps of Gandhi

"I want to realise brotherhood not merely with the beings called human, but with all life, even with such beings as crawl on the earth, because we claim a common descent from the same God." — Mahatma Gandhi

FROM GUJARAT WE travelled to the state of Maharashtra in central India, and to the city of Wardha, where Sevagram Ashram is situated. We were invited here by Siddharaj Dhadda, whom we had met in Jaipur, and who is a regular visitor and a member of this ashram.

"I spend at least half of my time here," said Siddharaj. "This is where Gandhi lived, and this place shows how Gandhi's mind worked. It is a model of a lifestyle closer to the natural elements and closer to the lives of ordinary people."

"How did this ashram begin?" I asked.

"Gandhi left his home on the banks of the Sabarmati River in Ahmedabad when he went on the Salt March," said Siddharaj. "At that time the British had imposed a tax on salt. In Gandhi's view that was utterly unjust. Salt was used by everyone, but a tax on salt would hit the poor hardest. Of course, as soon as Gandhi made salt he, along with thousands of his followers, were arrested and put in jail. This was the defining moment, a historic moment, the real start of the non-violent campaign to get the British out of India. Gandhi received tremendous support from around the world, including England itself, where Bertrand Russell among others took up the cause of India's freedom. When Gandhi came out of jail he met Jamnalal Bajaj, one of the wealthy merchants of Wardha, who had been deeply inspired by the action undertaken by Gandhi. Bajaj invited the Mahatma to make Wardha his home."

"And Gandhi accepted the invitation?" I interjected.

"Yes, he did," said Siddharaj. "In 1936, at the age of sixty-seven, he came to Wardha and chose a small village five miles away from the city. He renamed the place Sevagram ('village of service'); here he and his colleagues built a series of elegant earth houses and established the ashram. Every morning and evening they gathered together for prayer. Cooking, spinning, gardening, publishing and working for India's independence were their main activities; all of which they considered equally important. However busy he was, Gandhi would never allow a day to pass without participating in prayer and spinning. Also, every morning he would take a broom in his hands and clean the grounds as well as some of the village lanes. Sanitation was a passion too; he designed simple compost toilets which even the very poor could afford to build.

Siddharaj paused for a few seconds, and then said, "Gandhi explained his way of life thus: 'I am living now just the way I wish to live. What I might have done at the beginning had I had more light, I am doing now in the evening of my life: building from the bottom up.'

"Gandhi believed that we should *be* the change we want to see in the world. For Gandhi, his life was his message. As you know, when Gandhi was studying and then practising law in England and South Africa, he wore a Western suit. But when he began to organise people for the freedom struggle, he identified himself with them and gave up his suit. From then on he wore two unstitched pieces of cloth, just like the poorest peasants and workers."

"But why did he insist on mud huts?" I asked. "Why not some more permanent structures?"

Siddharaj replied, "The majority of people in Indian villages live in mud houses. Gandhi wanted to live like them. So he built a *kuti*, a simple earth hut, from the locally available natural materials—basically earth, wood and thatch."

Together we visited the hut, and it was a deeply moving experience. The hut is a profound statement in elegant simplicity and unpretentious beauty, built with love, lived in with love and now cared for with love. Love and simplicity are the abiding spirit of Gandhi's hut.

Siddharaj was overcome with emotion; his sincere and gentle voice became soft, his eyes moist. After clearing his throat, he continued:

"Gandhi believed that only right means could lead to right ends. How could he pursue the goals of simplicity, humility and equality while living in a house built with imported and factory-made materials? His home should be no different from the homes of the majority of Indians."

Siddharaj stretched out his arm and picked up a pamphlet, then he said,

"Once we invited Ivan Illich, the radical thinker and Jesuit, to Sevagram and he spoke here about the meaning of Gandhi's hut. Illich said, and I quote, 'This hut of Gandhi demonstrates to the world how the dignity of the common people can be brought up. It is also a symbol of the happiness we can derive from practising the principles of simplicity, service and truthfulness.' Illich understood Gandhi's mind."

"Once the ashram was established, then what happened?" I asked.

Siddharaj replied, "The Mahatma had a magnetic personality. He attracted great talents to come and live either at or near the ashram. Among them were many philosophers, economists, educationalists and spiritual seekers. Sevagram became the powerhouse not only for the freedom struggle but for the renewal of India through what Gandhi called the Constructive Programme. He declared that the people of India must replace the British system of centralised economic and political control. Instead they should build a decentralised local economy and a system of local governance where everyone could participate in politics. They should create a network of largely self reliant economies joined together by a web of co-operative relationships."

"Please explain the Constructive Programme," I requested.

Siddharaj replied, "The freedom struggle was, to some extent, a negative programme. It was a programme against colonialism and imperialism. In order to balance the negative nature of the campaign Gandhi presented a positive plan of action, which became known as the Constructive Programme, referring to what kind of economy and new social order would be created in place of the colonial system. The Constructive Programme included the promotion of small-scale workshops as opposed to large-scale factories; action to bring about an end to caste discrimination and untouchability; campaigns for gender equality; local economies; animal welfare, and so on. Gandhi pointed out that political independence would prove inadequate without social and economic transformation."

"But isn't it true that this vision has remained a dream?" I asked.

"In some ways it has," agreed Siddharaj, "but we must not forget that hundreds of thousands of workers gave up their well paid jobs and worked in the villages of India as part of the Constructive Programme, and they still do. Hundreds of young people are continuing to join the programme even today. However, I do agree that the programme did not succeed in the way Gandhi had envisaged—namely, a 'total revolution'."

"Why?" I asked.

"Because India became politically independent in 1947, but it was more a mirage of independence than true independence. And Gandhi never got the chance to realise his aspirations. Within six months he was assassinated, on January 30th, 1948. Without the force of Gandhi's imagination and without his charismatic leadership, those who took political power chose to pursue British-style industrialism and neglected the Constructive Programme."

Siddharaj was not going to stop on this pessimistic note. He said,

"However, after more than fifty years, here at Sevagram the ashram life still continues. Every morning at 4.30 a.m. as it always was, there is the multi-faith prayer composed by Gandhi himself. Ashram members still spin cotton, make cloth and grind grain on the same grindstones which Gandhi himself had used. The kitchen still maintains the tradition of communal living. Ashram members are still dedicated to a spiritual and egalitarian lifestyle. And Gandhians from all over India still come to be re-inspired at this place. The three great trees planted by Gandhi, his wife Kasturba and their colleague Vinoba are still here, spreading their branches over the ashram grounds and giving cool shade to the thousands of visitors. There is a tranquillity and serenity present here. All this gives me hope that the Gandhian spirit can rise again."

"Yet, there is something missing," I said. "The ashram seems to represent the great past but what about the future? Is Sevagram a place of nostalgia? Or of a new energy? It is a spiritual centre, but is it politically relevant?"

"There are some young Gandhians living at the ashram as well as around the country, who are challenging the status quo politically. They are campaigning for local self-government, local economies and freedom from the economic colonialism being fostered in the name of globalisation. Under the so-called liberalisation, Europeans and Americans get goods made in India at rock-bottom prices. This amounts to legalised theft from the poor. Furthermore, Western companies sell their goods in India at sky-high prices. This is called 'free trade'! When the exchange rate is so unfair, how can there be any talk of free trade? Gandhi and globalisation don't go together," Siddharaj said.

"Using India's cheap labour to manufacture goods for Western markets is a continuation of colonialism. International or global trade is all very well, but nobody cares about the squalid working conditions and unfair wages of the labourers. Giant global corporations are making vast profits on the back of grossly exploited Indian people. Though governments and corporations in the West talk about development and aid to the Third World, when they need doctors, nurses, teachers or computer programmers they seduce our most qualified young people with the lure of high salaries.

"They talk about feeding the hungry, but much of the most fertile land is used to grow animal feed for the meat industry of the West, and on what land is left they produce cash crops of tobacco, sugar, coffee and tea to support the addictions of the elite." Siddharaj spoke with passion.

I said, "Globalisation is supposed to be a way of reducing poverty!"

Siddharaj replied, "For the past fifty years every Indian and Western politician, every industrialist in India, America and Europe has spoken about the reduction of 'poverty'. But this is no more than deception. While they spoke about the 'poor' they made themselves even richer. The poor have been used as pawns to make the rich richer. Talking about the 'poor' is a ploy of the rich to create a smokescreen to hide their relentless pursuit of wealth. From the point of view of the peasants and the poor, we are witnessing the total failure of global economics and 'free trade'."

"What drives globalisation?" I asked.

"Globalisation is imposed on the world by the forces of capitalism, which is based on the principle of private ownership," answered Siddharaj. "Capitalists believe that humans have the right to own land, property and natural resources. The more they own, the greater their wealth.

"But among traditional societies there was no notion of ownership. Our distant ancestors did not consider themselves owners of nature. As tigers, elephants, horses, birds and other species were fed, watered and sheltered without owning the land or the forest, so were the native Americans, the bush people of the Kalahari and the Aboriginals of Australia. They flourished for thousands of years without owning the Earth. The native Americans believe that before we act, we must think, 'What will be the impact of our action on the seventh generation?' This is truly long-term thinking. This goes beyond the idea of private ownership of natural resources."

"How did the concept of ownership begin?" I asked.

"It began with the development of agriculture. But in those earlier times, the practice of ownership was not so damaging. People worked with hand tools, cultivated the land within walking distance and fished the oceans with small boats and small fishing nets. With such low impact technology, private ownership did not cause such huge problems.

"But now, with advanced technology, mass production, global commerce and speedy communication, the concept of private ownership threatens the survival of the Earth itself. Globalisation of trade is really privatisation of the commons, and now the idea of owning is even extended to include intellectual property rights. Already a large percentage of the world's resources, such as land, animals, forests, mines and water, is owned by a small number of individuals and corporations. With globalisation this ownership will be further concentrated in an even smaller number of hands. Why are 'the poor' poor? They are poor because all their sources of livelihood have been appropriated by the rich. This elite is educated, it holds the reins of power, and it is the maker of laws.

"In this context it is right to be questioning the very notion of ownership itself. We are part of the web of life, not the owners, nor even the managers nor the stewards; instead we should consider ourselves to be the trustees of the Earth."

"What do you mean by trustees?" I asked.

"The idea of trusteeship was first formulated by Mahatma Gandhi,"

answered Siddharaj. "He believed that we humans should hold the Earth
in sacred trust on behalf of all living beings and on behalf of future generations. It is the responsibility of a good trustee not to squander the original capital—only the interest can be spent, without depleting the capital.
Trustees are not allowed to use the money for their own personal advantage. They can receive expenses, which means that they can take what they
really need, but not more. Trustees must use the income of the trust for the
benefit of the general public."

Siddharaj continued, "In the capitalist system it is assumed that natural
resources are income or revenue, rather than capital. The fact that we call
them 'resources' shows that we consider them objects to be owned and
used. But, Gandhi believed that the Earth is our true capital and we are not
to deplete it. As trustees, we need to look for ways and means to replenish
and enhance rather than diminish the Earth. Only the renewable fruits of
the Earth can be shared among people and other creatures. Like an apple
tree giving apples, living creatures can of course enjoy the fruit, but not
destroy the tree itself. If we have to cut down a tree, it is our responsibility
to plant more trees than we have cut down. Trees, forests, rivers, mountains
and all other natural gifts are there to be shared for the continuation of life.
All creatures, humans and non-humans, should have access to the fruits of
the Earth. A small number of people should not own the natural capital and
exclude others from it: this leads to battles, revolutions and wars."

"But the advocates of ownership will argue that the concept of trusteeship will stifle initiative," I said.

"No," said Siddharaj. "A radical shift from ownership to trusteeship
will not preclude entrepreneurial or imaginative initiatives and ventures,
but such ventures will be less motivated by self-enrichment and self-seek-
ing, and more by the desire to serve and replenish the Earth. We need to
inject idealism, ethics and morality into our system; only then can we create a social and economic system which is fair and just."

"But people will ask, what is wrong with the system of ownership?"

"If we continue along the path of ownership and hope that all people—
six billion of us—can have equal access to the same resources, we will soon
be disappointed," said Siddharaj. "If everyone were to seek a Western standard of living, we would need the resources of four to five planets, which is
absurd. We need a new purpose in life which is different from the ideology
of high living standards for everyone. This new purpose could be termed
'trusteeship and elegant simplicity for everyone', where quality of life is more
important than quantity of possessions. 'Ownership' causes suffering, injustice, inequity and strife. Trusteeship is the way of justice, equity and harmony. Trusteeship reduces suffering and enables the renewal of the Earth."

I was delighted with this explanation. Siddharaj made Gandhi relevant to our present situation. Siddharaj was not looking backwards to Gandhi; he brought Gandhi forward to our time.

FROM SEVAGRAM WE walked to the village of Paunar. It was 6 a.m. The sun was rising. There was a cool breeze and mist over the fields of sugar cane, cotton, pulses, mustard and bananas. We walked along rich farmland irrigated by a canal. This was the path used by Vinoba when he visited Gandhi in Sevagram. In those days there was a dirt track, but now it has been tarmacked, which is hard on the feet. We walked at the side on the soft grass-covered earth.

After about an hour we arrived at a bridge over the River Dham, and crossed it to reach Vinoba's ashram. We were received by Kalindi, a woman who had been a close associate of Vinoba and now is one of the permanent members of the Ashram. Kalindi lives in a small, austere room surrounded by books, magazines and papers. It was to Kalindi that Vinoba told his life story, which she wrote down and edited into a book in Hindi, which later was translated into English by Marjorie Sykes and published under the title *Moved by Love.* [7]

"HOW DID VINOBA come to live here?" I asked Kalindi.

"In 1938, Vinoba's health deteriorated. Mahatma Gandhi said to him, 'Come and live at Sevagram. I will take care of you'.

" 'No, I won't come to Sevagram', replied Vinoba, 'because you have fifty other things to do and one of them is taking care of the sick. Then again, you have fifty other sick people to take care of. You won't have time to take care of me!'

" 'Yes, you are right. So go to see a doctor then.' requested Gandhi.

" 'I had rather see Death than see a doctor!' said Vinoba.

" 'Then go to some hill station for some rest and a change of air,' Gandhi pursued the matter.

" 'I won't go to a hill station either, but you are right that I should stay somewhere to rest and have a change of air. There is a house belonging to Bajaj by the banks of the River Dham. Bajaj has often suggested that I make use of that house. I will go there.'

"Gandhi was pleased. 'You are right not to go far away to an expensive hill station. Those places are not for ordinary people.' "

Continuing the story, Kalindi said, "This is how Vinoba came to Paunar. Not by design to start an ashram but to regain his health."

"But then how did the ashram start?" I asked.

"As Vinoba recovered through rest and recuperation," said Kalindi, "he started to work on the land as a means of exercise. The ground was full of stones, and digging was hard work. Yet he enjoyed it. One day he hit upon a large stone. He kept digging around it; it was much too big for him to move, so he sought assistance from others. When the stone was brought out of the ground, it became clear that it was no ordinary stone. It was an ancient image of Rama being greeted by his brother Bharata. This was a joyful, surprising and unexpected gift. Archaeologists later identified the place as the site of an old temple. Vinoba thought that he should stay here and take care of this gift. This is how the ashram began."

"DID VINOBA LIVE here by himself?" I asked.

"Only for a while", said Kalindi. "Once he had got better, he thought that this was as good a place as any to try a new way of living which would be economically viable and spiritually fulfilling. A group of dedicated young men gathered around him, and together they lived without money. They grew their own food, spun and wove their own clothes, made their own sandals, and if they needed anything from outside such as salt, kerosene oil or herbal medicine, they bartered it. They used no bullocks to plough the land: they pulled the plough themselves, both as a measure of economy and of non-violence to animals."

"Has that experiment continued?" I asked.

"No, not in the same way," said Kalindi. "The ashram has been through many changes over the years. Vinoba left for a while to join the Independence movement. And then he went away again to walk the length and breadth of India campaigning for Land Reform. Sometimes the number at the ashram dwindled, and at other times it swelled. But the spirit of the place remained vibrant. And then towards the end of the fifties the place became a women's ashram."

"This was a new departure, and quite different from the original idea of the ashram," I said.

"Yes," said Kalindi, "Vinoba had come to the conclusion that the future belongs to the feminine spirit and feminine power. There are many ashrams run by men, but none by women. So Vinoba offered this place to us women and thus a new chapter began."

"How does it work now?" I asked.

"Vinoba died in 1982, but he left the legacy of this great ashram to women. Some of us had walked with Vinoba and worked in the Land Reform movement. Four women had walked for twelve years across India, meeting people and inspiring them to remain true to their spiritual roots and the culture of India. Some have joined the Ashram subsequently. Now we are thirty-three women living here, practising celibacy, self-sufficiency, simplicity and studying sacred scriptures such as the *Gita* and other ancient and contemporary texts. Many women come from all over the country to stay here for a few weeks or longer, to share the life of the ashram members, and to study. When they return to their native place they use the skills and the experience gained here in their work of creating and building communities, and especially helping women and enabling their feminine qualities and skills to flourish," answered Kalindi.

Kalindi showed us around the garden, which Vinoba had started. "Years of mulching, compost and cultivation have made the soil rich and fertile. Every morning after breakfast Ashram members work in the garden," said Kalindi.

Then Kalindi showed us the ashram's *goshala* (cow sanctuary) and dairy. She also took us around the orchard, which was full of guavas, papayas, oranges, mangoes and bananas. We visited the printing works from where their journal, *Maitri* (Friendship), is printed and distributed. Similarly, books by Vinoba and other Gandhian writers are published here.

"What would you say was the unique quality of this ashram?" I asked.

"I would describe it as a place of collective spiritual practice which sustains the society at large."

"What does that mean?" I wondered.

"It means that instead of retiring to a monastery or mountain and seeking individual salvation, ashram members seek a social spirituality," replied Kalindi. "Personal transformation happens through social transformation, through service. We seek spiritual realisation not just for our own benefit but for the benefit of all. This is a particular emphasis of this place. In most ashrams people seek a higher state of consciousness as a personal journey of purity and self-development, but here at Paunar we live our lives in the world through serving others, working on the land, creating community, receiving guests, hosting conferences and working towards the eradication of social injustice. The world and God are not separate: God is in the world and the world is in God. Truth is God. Love is God. God is everywhere. God is here: we have to recognise the divinity of everything and live accordingly," she concluded.

THE INFLUENCE OF Gandhi and Vinoba on the city of Wardha and on the surrounding area is still strong. There are many innovative experiments and activities where rural renewal and community care are being carried out. One such project is '*Chetna*><*Vikas*' or 'Consciousness><Development' *

---

* Chetna><Vikas (Consciousness><Development) is written thus to imply that consciousness does and must have an impact on development, and vice versa.

a few miles outside Wardha, where work is initiated on the basis of being environmentally sound, socially just, culturally cohesive and economically sustainable. Niranjana, a young woman who works full-time on this project, said, "People's participation in the process of rural development—particularly that of women—is essential."

The project, after some research, has reintroduced the cultivation of traditional varieties of fruit tree. "They are a vital source of human nutrition, as well as providing food and shelter for wildlife," said Niranjana.

"Our aim is to give priority to the production of fruit for the local villagers, rather than export to distant markets," Niranjana added. "With the scarcity of land, the perennial crops of indigenous fruit trees have great potential to enhance the local economy." In addition to working towards a revolution in tree plantation, Chetna><Vikas is working to educate and inform village people about the value of organic farming, compost making, water conservation, animal husbandry and saving indigenous seeds and plants. "But this development work is carried out with the intention of making people aware of their own power. Without raising such consciousness, all development work leads to dependency and unsustainability," Niranjana insisted.

Besides Niranjana and her husband Ashok, there are other scientists who have come to live and work in the villages because they are committed to rural development. They are catalysts, training local women and men to be confident of indigenous knowledge. Their aim is not to impose an alien model of development, but to nurture the potential of local people and their skills.

AFTER BEING AWAY eighteen years, we returned to the Centre of Science for Villages where our son Mukti at the age of eight had spun a thousand yards of cotton on a spinning-wheel called Ambar Charkha. At that time we had been visiting Devendra Gupta and his wife Prabha. Devendra was one of those scientists who recognised the indigenous science of the villages and who committed himself to improving the living conditions of rural communities. Devendra always said that "For far too long science has been the preserve of the urban intellectual elite. Science is associated with highly educated people in white coats working in city laboratories. But this centre is rural. Here scientists are experimenting on simple theories to develop technologies which are appropriate to rural life and which are inexpensive."

After Devendra passed away his daughter Vibha, who has been educated in India and America, has continued with her father's work. On our arrival we were received by her. We sat on straw mats under a big tree where the staff were waiting. Cushions were also arranged for Vibha's father as if he were to attend the meeting in person. This symbolised the presence of his spirit and acknowledged the continuation of his work.

Vibha and her colleagues are working hard not only to keep Devendra's vision alive, but to take it forward. Vibha is in her late thirties, and is completely steeped in the work of rural revival. She has decided not to marry and have a family because that might distract her from the urgent task of bringing relief and renewal to rural India.

"Tell me more, Vibha," I asked, "about Devendra's vision for this centre."

"The Centre was established in 1976 to work towards a holistic and decentralised village economy; to arrest the migration of village talent to the cities; to provide a place for scientists who wished to work on village problems, to develop tools and techniques, and interact with village people," Vibha answered.

"What are the main activities of your centre?" I asked.

"The Centre researches, develops and promotes renewable energy, affordable housing, sanitation, village industries and sustainable agriculture. Here effective techniques of making bio-gas from slurry and sewage are demonstrated; simple smokeless stoves have been invented, and easy methods of organic composting, bio-fertilisers and natural pest deterrents are developed," explained Vibha.

"For example?" I asked.

"Village people rear goats, which damage the trees. After some research we found that the best goat-repellent was diluted goat urine, so we introduced methods of collecting the urine and spraying it on the tree saplings. This proved highly successful. The Centre has also looked into ways of honey production. Honey from domesticated beehives amounts to only 20% of the total honey harvested in India. The other 80% is made by wild bees in inaccessible places. Tribal and village honey hunters adopt crude methods of burning, smoking and squeezing the hives, which can lead to a loss of much of the honey and the death of the bee colonies. We have experimented and introduced safe methods of extracting wild honey without killing the bees. We spray the bees with water to deactivate them temporarily, and we use bamboo clips to prevent the hive from falling during extraction. These techniques enable honey collectors to complete the process causing neither waste nor harm. We have trained over 1,000 people in these skills," she said.

Vibha disproves the stereotype of Indian women as powerless and subservient. She not only manages the project itself but also provides training to village people. Moreover, she and her colleagues take their work to the villagers and offer it to them at minimal cost.

Vibha, like Kalindi and Niranjana, showed that much good work is being done by the women of India, and they are following in the footsteps of Mahatma Gandhi with total commitment and dedication.

Chapter 24

Seeds of Renewal

VANDANA SHIVA IS another example of a woman creating a revolution at the grass roots. We met her at New Delhi station before dawn. She was wearing an olive green sari with a broad black border and a shawl casually thrown over her shoulders. A large round red mark (*bindi*) had been placed on her forehead between the eyebrows at the place of the third eye, and her long black hair was bound in a plait. Vandana radiated an aura of grace, warmth, energy and confidence. We felt excited to be travelling with her to her home town of Dehra Dun.

Vandana is a fearless and passionate campaigner for the land, forests, women, countryside, small farmers, biodiversity, indigenous values and right livelihood. A peaceful warrior against the onslaught of economic globalisation, the dominance of multinational corporations, the industrialisation of agriculture and the commercialisation of basic human necessities such as food, water and shelter, she is a saver of seeds and a conserver of cultures.

Having studied both philosophy and physics, Vandana is able to marry traditional with modern attitudes and seek a synthesis between the rational mind and the feeling heart. In consequence she is as much an activist as a scientist, and able to back her intuitions with empirical evidence.

Vandana's spacious family home, built by her father, is situated in about an acre of land and surrounded with beautiful old trees. The house now belongs to all members of the family, her brother, her sister and their children. Part of the time Vandana spends in Delhi organising campaigns in support of small-scale, sustainable farming, and the other part in Dehra Dun where she does her teaching, research and writing.

Over a cup of tea on the veranda we started to talk about the famous forest resistance, known as the 'Hug the Trees movement', led by women including Vandana.

"What was the occasion which precipitated that resistance?" I asked.

"In the seventies, the central government in New Delhi and the state government in Lucknow had given licence to the logging companies to cut down large parts of the Himalayan forest, which provided food, fodder, shelter and livelihood to local people," said Vandana. "When the devastating news of this commercial project reached the region, the women got together and planned to stop the loggers. Time was against them. There was no possibility to contact government officials nor to engage in any formal protest, so they simply decided to 'Hug the Trees'. They resolved to remain by the trees until the loggers left the area."

"How did they do it?" I asked.

"The women—hundreds of them—tied themselves to the trees. They sang songs and chanted mantras to honour the forest. There was neither hatred, nor anger, nor abuse. The women simply said, 'Trees are our bodies, if you wish to cut down the trees, your chainsaws have to go through our bodies. We will live or die with our trees. We are born in the forest, we live with the forest and we will die for the forest.' "

"What was the reaction of the loggers?" I asked.

"They were stunned and surprised. They did not know what to do. They waited for days in the hope that the women's patience would run out. But little did they know that these Himalayan women have a Himalayan resolve! Days and nights passed. Women organised a rota for being in the embrace of the trees. Men organised a support system to cook and feed the women as well as the children and themselves. The protest turned into a festival," said Vandana. "The occasion proved a training ground and a learning opportunity for many of us. Eventually the loggers and their chainsaws were defeated. Their trucks arrived empty and returned empty. The women won the battle of the forests. They saved their livelihood and their culture while saving their trees," she concluded.

FROM DEHRA DUN we travelled to Vandana's farm, some ten miles outside the city in the foothills of the Himalayas, surrounded by mango groves and natural forest. Here she has acquired ten acres of land on which she has established a centre for research, experiment, study and living called the International College for Sustainable Living (Bija Vidya Peeth). It offers an education for Earth citizenship through the knowledge of 'seeds, seasons and soil'. Courses are held on how to ensure sustainable and ecological food production and how to set up seed banks and seed networks. For Vandana, seeds are the symbols of self-reliance and sustainability.

Other themes include holistic science, organic farming, sustainable cities, Gandhi and globalisation, and learning from the South. The courses are open to foreign as well as Indian participants.

"How different is your research from that of the universities and government institutions?" I asked.

"Our research is not done in a vacuum," said Vandana, "as it is designed to be relevant to the lives of people. Universities carry out academic research in the abstract and impose their findings on people. This is how the disastrous 'Green Revolution' was brought about, and that is how genetically engineered seeds are now being imposed on farmers. Establishment scientists and the farmers live in two different worlds. Most scientists are cut off from the realities on the ground. Our research is based on the land and the people working on it. Here village people themselves participate in the researching, gathering data and analysing it.

"We are concerned with measuring and evaluating the success of traditional methods of farming, such as crop combining. We monitor the food value yielded by a variety of different plants growing together, as compared with the food value of mono-crops."

"What kinds of activity have you undertaken?" I asked.

"For example," said Vandana, "we are examining how two acres of land can best sustain a family of six, deriving their nourishment from leaves, fruit, roots and grains suited to the local climate and soil conditions. Our research has revealed that through local knowledge of food production, people are better able to feed themselves than if they have 'scientific' interference from outside. Local skills, local knowledge and local information have accumulated and developed over the millennia, based on long-term experiment and experience of the successes and failures of particular methods."

Vandana and her colleagues are recording the knowledge of local people which the scientific establishment has ignored. "Local knowledge of farming and forestry maintains diversity," said Vandana, "and diversity is the mother of abundance—whereas academic science insists on mono-crops, the cause of scarcity. The system of diversity reveals that when one crop fails there are other crops to provide sustenance—whereas in the mono-crop system, the failure of one crop means the failure of the whole harvest; there is nothing to fall back on."

Vandana further observed, "Diversity has been the basis of traditional Indian agriculture. There are thousands of varieties of indica rice alone which grow in India, and then there are thousands of varieties of millet, pulses and cereals that have nourished our vast population for millennia. Traditional farming systems have always practised mixed cropping, rotations and green manuring. Even on small plots of land, trees like neem and plants like perennial basil (*tulsi*) have been used as a protection against pests and diseases."

This was not just theory; we experienced the fruit of diversity during our meal. The farm kitchen offered us a delicious lunch of five kinds of bread made from five different grains, and vegetables which were specific to this particular locality, not being found anywhere else. We wondered why the whole of India was suddenly eating the same few varieties of rice and wheat and vegetables when there was such a treasure of local varieties available in every corner of the country.

While we savoured our lunch, Vandana continued to talk. "In the epic legend of Ramayana, Lord Rama, together with his wife Sita and his brother Lakshman, go into exile for twelve years and live in the forest. Not for a second do they worry about what they will eat in the wilderness. Hundreds of varieties of fruit, nuts, berries, beans, roots were easily at hand, in every nook and cranny of the forest."

"And Indian culture is very much a forest culture," I observed.

"Yes, because the sages of India have for millennia lived in the forests," said Vandana. "They cultivated no gardens, hunted no animals, and lived on wild fruits of the forest while meditating on nature, learning from nature and teaching their students about the mystery of nature."

"Traditional Indian medicine (ayurveda) is based on the roots and fruits of the forest," I commented.

"Very much so," said Vandana. "When novices came to the teachers of ayurveda, who lived in the forests, to learn about the medicinal and healing qualities of herbs, they learnt about the medicinal properties of every plant in the forest. After many years of their studies, when they were ready to go back to their communities to practise medicine, the teacher would ask them to go to the forest and look for a plant with no healing properties. Those students who returned having found no such plant would be accepted as fully qualified practitioners. But those who came back with a plant whose healing properties they did not know, would be asked to continue their studies!" Then she went on, "Indian forests are a treasure house of food and medicine. Rural people knew how to use the abundantly available nutrients of the forest plants, and the knowledge was handed down to them from generation to generation, but now that knowledge is fast disappearing under the influence of mono-crops and factory-made synthetic medicine. I call it monoculture of the mind."

Changing the subject, Vandana commented on the present predicament of the Indian farmers. "Thousands of peasants and farmers are committing suicide because they cannot pay their debts and cannot feed their families. The globalisation of the food trade is the tyranny of our time. We thought we had put slavery, holocausts, and apartheid behind us, but the globalisation of the food trade is imposing a new kind of slavery, a new kind of holocaust and a new kind of apartheid. Global trade is a war against nature, women and family farmers; war against diversity, smallness and local economies. Centralised, globalised, large-scale monoculture farming is violent farming. Small-scale, decentralised, diverse and local farming is non-violent farming."

"Large-scale agribusiness looks at crops, at animals, at water and forests, and sees them as commodities," I said.

"Yes, even people become commodities," said Vandana. "They get called 'human resources'. Whereas those who live on the land and work in harmony with the seasons and the conditions of the land see life and its nourishment as a gift. The culture of commodity and the culture of gift are at odds with each other. The culture of commodity perceives living beings as things, and living nature as merely a resource to be exploited for economic profit."

Upon this world-view Vandana Shiva's life and work is based. Through campaigning, research and teaching she is developing the practice and philosophy of the gift economy and spreading her knowledge among others.

AFTER SPENDING THE night at Dehra Dun we travelled to Rishikesh, a tranquil town on the banks of the river Ganges. We had to leave our car on the west side and cross the river over a footbridge to the east side where no cars can gain access. All supplies and building materials are carried on foot or by boat. House after house has been dedicated to pilgrims, priests and ascetics who come here to find peace of mind and salvation of soul. We saw bathers immersing themselves in the holy waters of the Ganges, chanting, "O, Mother River, you clean my body, my mind and my soul. As I am immersed in your water I relinquish my anguish and attachment, my greed and pride; take them away with you in your flowing waters and free me from my fears and fantasies."

Legend has it that the Ganges was the river of heaven, flowing across the astral plains, nourishing the stars and the planets. Once upon a time King Bhagirath prayed to the Gods to let the Ganges come to the Earth so that the holy waters of the river could bring fertility to the drought-stricken people of his kingdom. The Gods of compassion, pleased with the sincere prayers of the king, agreed to send the Ganges to the Earth, but warned him that the Earth might not be able to bear the force of the mighty river. Then the king went to Shiva, the God of the Himalayas, and urged him to let the Ganges come to Earth through his thick, heavy, matted hair so that the Earth would not be damaged by the powerful flow of her descent. Shiva was pleased to oblige the king and let the heavenly river flow through the forest of his hair, and over the valleys of his body.

Thus the river appears at Gangotri, which stands 3,000 metres above sea level in the Himalayas and is called Bhagirathi River after the king, until it reaches the plains at Rishikesh. All rivers are daughters of the

Ganges, and therefore all are holy for the Hindus, but the Ganges is the Mother, the Holy of Holies, the cleanser of impurities, healer of pains, destroyer of sufferings, giver of joy, source of harmony and provider of prosperity.

From Rishikesh we drove to the city of Haridwar, which means 'gateway to the Gods'. Here many ashrams are offering courses in Sanskrit studies, healing through chanting, yoga, meditation and much more. On the banks of the river we acquired a small palm leaf boat filled with marigold flowers with a candle at its centre. A priest blessed it for us, lit the candle and we then settled it on the waters and watched it floating until it disappeared among the waves.

Hundreds of other pilgrims did the same. With this ritual, the temple at Harki Pairi becomes a magnet, every evening drawing thousands of people to witness the river, which is alight with floating candles and adorned with the rainbow colours of floating flowers. This brief glimpse of Rishikesh and Haridwar rekindled our sense of wonder.

*   *   *

You cannot solve problems with the way
of thinking that led to their creation.

—Albert Einstein

PART FOUR

A Relational Philosophy

"I think, therefore I am."
—René Descartes

Sowing the seed
my hand is one with the earth.

Wanting the seed to grow,
my mind is one with the light.

Hoeing the crop,
my hands are one with the rain.

Having cared for the plants,
my mind is one with the air.

Hungry and trusting,
my mind is one with the earth.

Eating the fruit,
my body is one with the earth.

—Wendell Berry

Chapter 25

You Are, Therefore I Am:
A Reverential Ecology

"What pattern connects the crab to the lobster and the orchid to the primrose and all four of them to me? And me to you? And all the six of us to the amoeba in one direction and the backward schizophrenic in another? What is the pattern which connects all living creatures?"
—Gregory Bateson

'I THINK, THEREFORE I AM' (*Cogito, ergo sum*), proclaimed René Descartes. This one phrase describes the direction of Western science, philosophy, politics and the social order. When I first heard it, I was puzzled by Cartesian logic; in India we have been speaking of the dissolution and even the non-existence of the self for many centuries. But here was an eminent European philosopher basing the very foundation of existence on the self!

As I learnt more about Western culture, I realised how Cartesian dualism was an essential feature of a thought process which divided mind and matter, separated soul and body and looked at the world as a collection of objects to be analysed, compartmentalised, classified, and controlled. This Cartesian subject-object dualism or mind-matter split has become the dominant paradigm of Western culture.

It is interesting to note that Descartes had his philosophical insight while literally sitting in a stove, in an isolated and lonely place, whereas the Buddha had his enlightenment sitting under a tree, by a river, observing nature. No wonder the Buddha saw reality as 'co-dependent arising', which could be roughly translated as 'Only Connect'.

Descartes attracted everybody's attention because he was the first philosopher to bring scientific methodology into philosophical investigation. The starting point of Cartesian enquiry is doubt, which was a useful tool at a time when questioning was quashed and blind beliefs imposed. But Cartesian doubt went too far—the baby was thrown out with the bath water.

My upbringing was rooted in faith and in trust. Descartes discarded trust altogether, and a new dogma of doubt and then dualism became the dominant paradigm of his thinking, and later of Western culture.

Of course Descartes was not the first dualist. Its origins lie in the story of Genesis, in which God is separate from the world; God created the world and then He created Man in His own image, and gave humans dominion over the Earth. He instructed Man to subdue the Earth and multiply. Yet not all Christians interpreted the story in this way. The Celts saw the presence of God in creation itself and not outside it, and mystic Christians experienced the divine mystery present all around them. Nevertheless, the dominant Judaeo-Christian influence, which informed the affairs of state, the minds of the educated and the activities of trade, technology, art and science, was dualistic.

In order to accomplish the materialistic ambitions of the eighteenth-, nineteenth- and twentieth-century elites, it was necessary to marginalise the mystic and non-dualistic Christians, and to push upon mainstream Christians Cartesian philosophy, Newtonian physics, Darwinian biology and Freudian psychology, so that religion went hand in hand with the colonial, industrial and political designs of the European rulers of the time.

Newton saw the universe as a machine, a sophisticated clock which could be controlled and regulated to human needs. In his view, human and animal bodies were also machines. Animals, according to Descartes, had no soul, no feelings and no consciousness; the universe was not a living organism. The only thing required in order to manipulate it was to understand the laws of nature. Darwin's theory of Evolution developed the notion that species and individuals within species are in constant competition with each other, that strong species dominate the weak, and that only the strongest survive. The implication is that the only thing we need to do is become strong, and then we will be the master species. Similarly, in the field of psychology Freud seems to suggest that the psyche is wrapped in the skin, separate from the body; that the self can be accessed through analysis, and that by strengthening the ego the individual can gain power. All these ideas are centred around the self, and maintain a dualistic perspective.

These theories are, in my view, at the root of the ecological, social and spiritual crisis of our time. The dualistic world-view gives the illusion that I exist independently of the Other. This attitude is founded on the belief that there is a substantial, separate, individual Self, which can act of its own accord, irrespective of the Other. Once we accept that mind is more certain than matter and 'My mind' is more certain than the 'Other mind', we have already divided the world.

This is Separational Philosophy.

THERE ARE OTHER PHILOSOPHIES which seek the whole beyond the parts. They see the tree as a tree, and not as a collection of trunk, branches, leaves, flowers, fruit. They see the forest as a forest and not a collection of different kinds of trees, animals, birds, insects, streams and other life forms. They look at the world and see it whole. Species are not in competition but in symbiotic relationship. Life on Earth is not a fight for survival; rather the Earth nurtures life—it is a life-enhancing home. Mutuality and reciprocity are the underlying principles of existence. Wherever there is reciprocity, there is relationship. All species are members of one Earth community.

Here are examples of such Relational Philosophies:

The Jains say, "All is in the giving." The sun gives light to the plant, the plant gives fruit to the birds, birds distribute the seed, the seeds give themselves to the earth, and earth gives life to the seed.

The Buddhists call this phenomenon 'co-dependent arising'. When the sun rises, green shoots appear, leaves unfurl, flowers bud and fruit is formed. With the sun, birds rise; with the sun, people rise; all rise together. Everyone's rising depends on everyone else's rising. When Buddha understood this he was enlightened, and attained Nirvana, a state of liberation. But he said that there can be no Nirvana for one person until all beings are enlightened. We rise and fall together; ultimately, we all sink or swim together. We are inter-beings. "To be is to inter-be." We cannot be by ourselves alone. This means our being is only possible because of other beings. We are not individual beings; we are world beings.

In parts of Africa there is a word 'umbutu', meaning 'we are'. There is no such thing as 'I am' nor 'it is', always 'we are'; we are a web of relationships. It does not just refer to humanity; it means the whole of existence is together, interlinked, totally connected. The Native Americans call it Earth family; sky-father, earth-mother, ocean-grandmother, buffalo-brother.

Hindus say "So Hum"—'You are, therefore I am' (Estis, ergo sum). I did not drop from the sky, I was born of a mother: mother is, therefore I am. I learned much from the teachings of the Buddha, Mahavir, Jesus, Mohammed—these great teachers are, therefore I am. I am fed by the fruits of the Earth, the sun gives me warmth, water moistens me, I breathe air. These elements are, therefore I am. I am influenced and inspired by Gandhi, Tolstoy, Tagore and Van Gogh. My ancestors are, therefore I am.

THERE IS NO separate, isolated, disconnected self. Things appear separate if we see them as separate, they appear related when we see them as related. It is all in the seeing. Seers see the whole. Unlike Descartes, who believed the soul to live in the pineal gland, St Thomas Aquinas saw that the soul is not in the body, but the body is in the soul. We are part of the *anima mundi*, the world soul.

There can be no individual person without the context of community, environment, tradition and culture. Individuality and universality are complementary. Non-dualism is not a denial of individuality, it is to see individuality in the context of universality.

The consequence of Cartesian dualism is to put individuals in opposition to each other and the world at large, making life a battleground. Every individual has to fend for herself or himself, and the individual engages in actions for his or her own benefit. Individualism gives birth to exploitation of the weak by the strong, fights for power and wealth, subjugation of animals and nature, and the ultimate frustration of an unfulfilled and meaningless life.

In Separational Philosophy the individual is encouraged to take, take, take, and this ceaseless taking leads to nothing but anxiety. We live in anxious times: fear, insecurity and mistrust rule our lives. This is because we have lost the way of deep relationship with the Other, and our sense of belonging to a place and a community. The struggle for power and wealth has been with us since we left the garden of Eden. This is not a new phenomenon. But in earlier times the values of tribes, communities, families and religions enabled and supported an ethos of reciprocity and mutuality rather than the tendencies to control and dominate. But now, in the age of modernity and materialism, the values of relational thinking have been swept away, and aggressive attitudes are respected.

To remedy the situation we need to return to the notion of 'only connect'. All existence is a participatory process. To see the relationships which are the basis of life is to see the whole picture. Nothing can really be understood without its context and its relatedness to other things. When we wish to know someone we have to know their family background, their history, their education, their culture, their habits, their friends, their interests, their environment and so on. No person is an island. Even an island is an island only in relationship to the water surrounding it.

When someone is sitting in the sunshine drinking a cup of tea, do we see a collection of individual items or a pattern of relationships? This event is the coming together of the person, the drink, the weather and the place. The drink itself is a coming together of the cup, the water and the tea leaves, beyond which are the growers of the tea and the makers of the cup. As we look deeper and deeper we find an intricate, complex, creative and seemingly chaotic web of relationships. It is all relationships. Gregory Bateson said that a hand does not comprise five fingers, it comprises four relationships. Thomas Berry said that the universe is not a collection of objects, it is a communion of subjects.

In the relational paradigm, the individual receives from the universe at large. As Jesus said, "Consider the lilies of the field, how they grow, they toil not neither do they spin." We are all givers and receivers. This leads to caring for each other, and nurturing the earth, because ultimately there is no distinction between the Earth and ourselves.

Separational Philosophy leads to a position of either 'one' or the 'other'. Either individualism or collectivism, either materialism or spirituality, either art or science, either reductionism or holism, either humanism or environmentalism—whereas Relational Philosophy equips us to recognise the reality of 'both . . . and . . .'. Individual and society are two sides of the same coin. Matter and spirit exist together; art and science complement each other; we need a reductionist approach where appropriate and within the context of the whole. We need rationalism in balance with intuition and emotion. Life is not a battleground, not a sphere of conflict; rather, life is a ground of symbiotic relationships, where even battles and conflicts have a place, as do compassion and harmony.

IN THE PRESENT day, conflict and strife dominate. 11th September 2001 was a prime example of the world at war with itself. I was in New York on that day, staying in Greenwich Village, only a couple of miles from the World Trade Centre. I was with my friend Ron Williams. When we heard the loud sirens of emergency vehicles we came out of the house and stood at the crossroads of Seventh Avenue and Bleeker Street. I could not believe my eyes, what I was witnessing. I had to hold Ron in an embrace to contain myself. The south tower was on fire and people were already jumping out of the windows into the open sky. Moments later I saw an aeroplane circling round the north tower, then moving away from it, turning towards it and after gathering momentum plunging into the tower. A huge fireball erupted, the like of which I could never have imagined. An enormous black mushroom of smoke and dust clouded the sky and darkened the day, which had been so bright and sunny. The pictures of the mushroom rising above Hiroshima came to my mind. I saw the towers collapsing. Cries of "Oh my God", "Oh my God" rose from the thousands who stood in the street, witnessing the horror.

It is easy to condemn the terrorists, which of course every nation, every politician and every commentator duly did. There is no justification for involving one group of innocent civilians to kill other civilians. It is also easy to preach peace to terrorists, but such condemnation and preaching is not going to be effective unless the strong, powerful and wealthy nations begin to practise the non-dualistic principles of peace and non-violence themselves.

The government of the USA, and the policies of self-interest it is pursuing, are being questioned and criticised by many around the world, and by some wise citizens of the USA itself. For example, Paul Kennedy of Yale University wrote:

"We comprise slightly less that 5% of the world's population, but we imbibe 27% of the world's annual oil production, create and consume nearly 30% of its gross product, and—get this—spend a full 40% of *all* the world's defence expenditure. By my calculation, the Pentagon's budget is nowadays roughly equal to the defence expenditure of the next nine or ten highest defence spending nations, which has never before happened in history. That is indeed a heavy footprint. How do we explain it to others and to ourselves?"

In truth, there is no explanation. The 400 billion dollars which the US government is spending annually on 'defence' is to defend an unjust and unsustainable 'American Way of Life' which is otherwise indefensible.

The US government and other wealthy nations of the world have to ask: "What have we done to anger these people so much, that they are prepared to kill themselves and thousands of others in order to be heard, and to express their grievances?" The questions of equity and justice are paramount in the minds of those who are oppressed, exploited and deprived. There is a large number of people around the world who are in that bracket. For too long these questions have been swept under the carpet, in the belief that on the one hand, dissent can be put down by the might of the military and police, and on the other hand, that dissatisfaction can be diverted by the handouts of aid, the trickle-down from economic growth, the temptation of consumer goods and the crumbs of development falling from the tables of the rich.

11th September has proved that nuclear weapons and billions of dollars spent on defence are no guarantee for security. Equally, the distant mirage of a consumer lifestyle for the underprivileged is no compensation for the present hardship, suffering and injustice faced by billions of people. One way or another they are going to get angry and rebel.

What is the fundamental cause of conflict, highlighted by 11th September but in evidence all around the world? It is the paradigm that all individuals, families, communities, classes, societies and nations must seek their own, separate self-interest.

The Marxist class analysis is very much based on dualism; on the notion that different groups of people have their own different interests. Therefore, the interest of the working class is in conflict with the interest of the ruling class. Marx's solution is armed revolution. The history of class struggle is embedded in the same dualistic paradigm as that of René Descartes and Adam Smith.

Whether it is capitalism or communism, both emerge from the same idea that the pursuit of self-interest is a natural force which drives history forward and brings about progress and development. But if we are ruled by this belief there can be no end to conflict.

As many of my teachers and mentors about whom I have written in this book have taught me, we need to move from the motivation of self-interest to the recognition of common interest. Ultimately all creatures, humans and other than humans, wish to live, flourish and prosper. Therefore, we all need each other's help and love.

Even the environmental movement, which aspires to protect the Earth, is often driven by a pragmatic, utilitarian, dualistic and anthropocentric world-view. 'The Environment' is out there and we need to protect it because humankind cannot survive without good soil, clean air and pure water. The survival of the human species is a broad enough concept, but still it is limited. Prioritising human interests becomes a pretext for safeguarding American interests, British interests, Indian interests and other national interests. This is a kind of selfish ecology, the roots of which are still in the Cartesian mode of dualism. The unity of life is not just about human survival, it is about a deep respect and reverence for all life. The need is not only to protect or conserve nature, but to recognise the sanctity of all life. This is Reverential Ecology. When we need to take other lives for our survival we must do so with humility, care and restraint rather than thinking that it is our right to take other lives.

A passionate single-minded concern for nature can even reinforce the separation between nature and people. If ecologists ensure that reverence remains an essential aspect of their philosophy, then there will be no need to separate people from nature. Without reverence there can be no ecology, and without spirituality there can be no sustainability. Unless we are prepared to make a radical shift in our thinking and act accordingly, we will not be able to bring an equilibrium between conflict and harmony, and attain wholeness.

* * *

Chapter 26

A Declaration of Dependence

"We are here to awaken from the illusion of our separateness."
—Thich Nhat Hanh

THE AMERICAN DECLARATION of Independence in 1776 may have been right in its time and context. At times of slavery, colonialism and imperialism, it is right and proper that the colonised stand up for their dignity and claim freedom from oppression.

But now the age of Ecology is dawning and a new consciousness is being born. In the wake of multiple environmental crises, we are rediscovering the ancient wisdom that we depend on each other and we depend on the ways of nature. We depend on the Earth.

The Industrial Revolution, scientific discoveries and technological inventions have created the illusion that we, the human race, are the rulers, that we can take nature's laws into our own hands, and do what we like with them. We are the masters of creation; we are in charge of the natural world—its forests, rivers, mountains, fishes, fossils, animals, birds, oil, gas, coal. We have dominion over the land, the oceans and the sky. We can split the atom, engineer genes and walk upon the moon. We can ever diminish the wild, enslave the animals, dam the rivers and deplete the energy reserves accumulated over millennia. There are no limits to our power.

This is human arrogance at its worst. As a result we have turned the abundant bounty of natural gifts into scarcity. Time is infinite, yet we have turned it into a limited commodity. We have reduced the Earth, our planet, our home, to a battlefield where we are competing and fighting for materials, markets and power.

NOW WE ARE at a crossroads. We can continue to follow the same path. We can continue to live in the illusion of perpetual economic growth. We can stick to our technological addiction. We can pursue genetics, robotics, nano- and nuclear technology. We can take the road to ruin. We can drive

to the abyss. Or we can turn towards ecology: the path of values, ethics
and aesthetics, the path of love and reverence for nature, the path of participatory science. We can relinquish the knowledge which enables us to
lord it over the Earth. Like the Chinese in the middle ages, who discovered
gunpowder but decided to use it only for fireworks, we can be wise and say
enough is enough.

For survival and for the good life we need humility. We come from the
soil and will return to the soil. We are part of nature, neither above it nor
separate from it. Nature is the source of all life: the source of joy and celebration, the source of arts and imagination, the source of poetry and
inspiration, the source of skills and inventions. Earth gives us experience of
time and space, it gives us seasons and change. We work and rest in
response to the earthly cycles. Earth grants us a sense of place, from which
we derive our identity and belonging. Earth is the source of music, dance
and delight. It is the source of beauty, wisdom and insight. For our existence and experience, for our happiness and health, for our nutrition and
nourishment, we depend on the Earth. We depend on the love of the
beloved, the beauty of the beautiful and the goodness of the good.
Embracing vulnerability and humility, let us declare our utter dependence
on the Earth, and on each other: You are, therefore I am.

*   *   *

Because We Are.

I am because we are, the five-toed,
the elegant-fingered, the ones
whose brains flower like coral
whose dreams span earth and move out—
I am because we animals
love to rub and huddle, because
our tongues love to lick skin,
nuzzle and enter each other's
mouths, clean milky young,
taste sweat from necks and slick
fur flat, lap water from clean pools:
because we love to swim, sleep, eat,
lie in the sun, move to the shade;
and because we are the fish
flying in ballets through shallows
and deeper, where the ocean floor
hollows and darkness begins;
I am because of centuries of thought
and centuries of dream, because of poetry,
grass, music, growing corn,
because of wine from grapes
and bread from flour,

because of a million hands,
because of cave paintings
and the true line drawn,
the bison on the wall,
doe in the clearing, because
of shooting stars and sudden floods,
ships going out, footprints,
because of men and women
coming together, lying down
together, coming, again and again,
because of father, mother, brothers,
lovers, children, everyone making
enough love, because of skins, eyes, hands
and words, because of closeness,
because of breath. Because
of the touch in the night
the surgeon who saved me
because of intelligence
because of care
because of enough people
loving enough people
for those centuries
for ever, I am. We.

—Rosalind Brackenbury

Notes

1. Umasvati & Nathmal Tatia (translator), *That Which Is*, Introduction, HarperCollins 1994.

2. S. Radhakrishnan, *Indian Philosophy*, OUP New Delhi 1999.

3. For my description of leaving home and becoming a monk see *No Destination: an autobiography*, Green Books, new edition 2000.

4. Vinoba Bhave, *Talks on the Gita*, Sarva Seva Sangh Prakashan, Rajghat, Varanasi, 221001 India, <www:mkgandhi-sarvodaya.org>.

5. Ishavasyopanishad in *The Ten Principal Upanishads* translated by Purohit Swami and W. B. Yeats, Faber and Faber, London 1937.

6. Nirmal Verma, 'An Unwritten Epic' in *Resurgence* 187, March–April 1988.

7. The full story of Vinoba's life is described in his memoirs, *Moved by Love*, Green Books 1994.

8. For further explanation see *Talks on the Gita* (note 4 above).

9. The full text of Krishnamurti's speech about dissolving the Order of the Star of the East is published in *Total Freedom: The Essential Krishnamurti*', Harper San Francisco.

10. Barth, *The Religions of India*, pp.148–150.

11. Gospel according to St Matthew, Chapter 19 Verse 24.

12. E. F. Schumacher, 'Conscious Culture of Poverty' in *This I Believe*, Green Books 1997, p.81.

13. *Open Secret: Versions of Rumi*, Threshold Books, Vermont 1986, p.13.

14. Ibid., p.21.

Index

Resurgence

Satish Kumar is Editor of Resurgence magazine, described in *The Guardian* as "the spiritual and artistic flagship of the green movement". If you would like a sample copy of a recent issue, please contact:

Jeanette Gill, Rocksea Farmhouse,
St. Mabyn, Bodmin, Cornwall PL30 3BR
Telephone & Fax 01208 841824 www.resurgence.org

He is also Director of Programmes at Schumacher College, an international centre for ecological studies. For the latest course programme, please contact:

The Administrator, Schumacher College
The Old Postern, Dartington, Totnes, Devon TQ9 6EA
Telephone 01803 865934 Fax 01803 866899
www.schumachercollege.org

Also available from Green Books:

NO DESTINATION
An autobiography

Satish Kumar

"One of the few life-changing books I have ever read. I wish everyone would read it."—Thomas Moore, author of *Care of the Soul*

"Reading this book, you will have the rare pleasure of meeting a warm and witty, thoroughly genuine man, and one whose inspiration will not fail to move you."—Kirkpatrick Sale, author of *Rebels Against the Future*

320pp 216 x 138mm ISBN 1 870098 89 7 £9.95 paperback